AIRCRAFT OF THE ACES

127

POLISH SPITFIRE ACES

BL860
T

SERIES EDITOR TONY HOLMES

127 AIRCRAFT OF THE ACES

Wojtek Matusiak and Robert Grudzień

POLISH SPITFIRE ACES

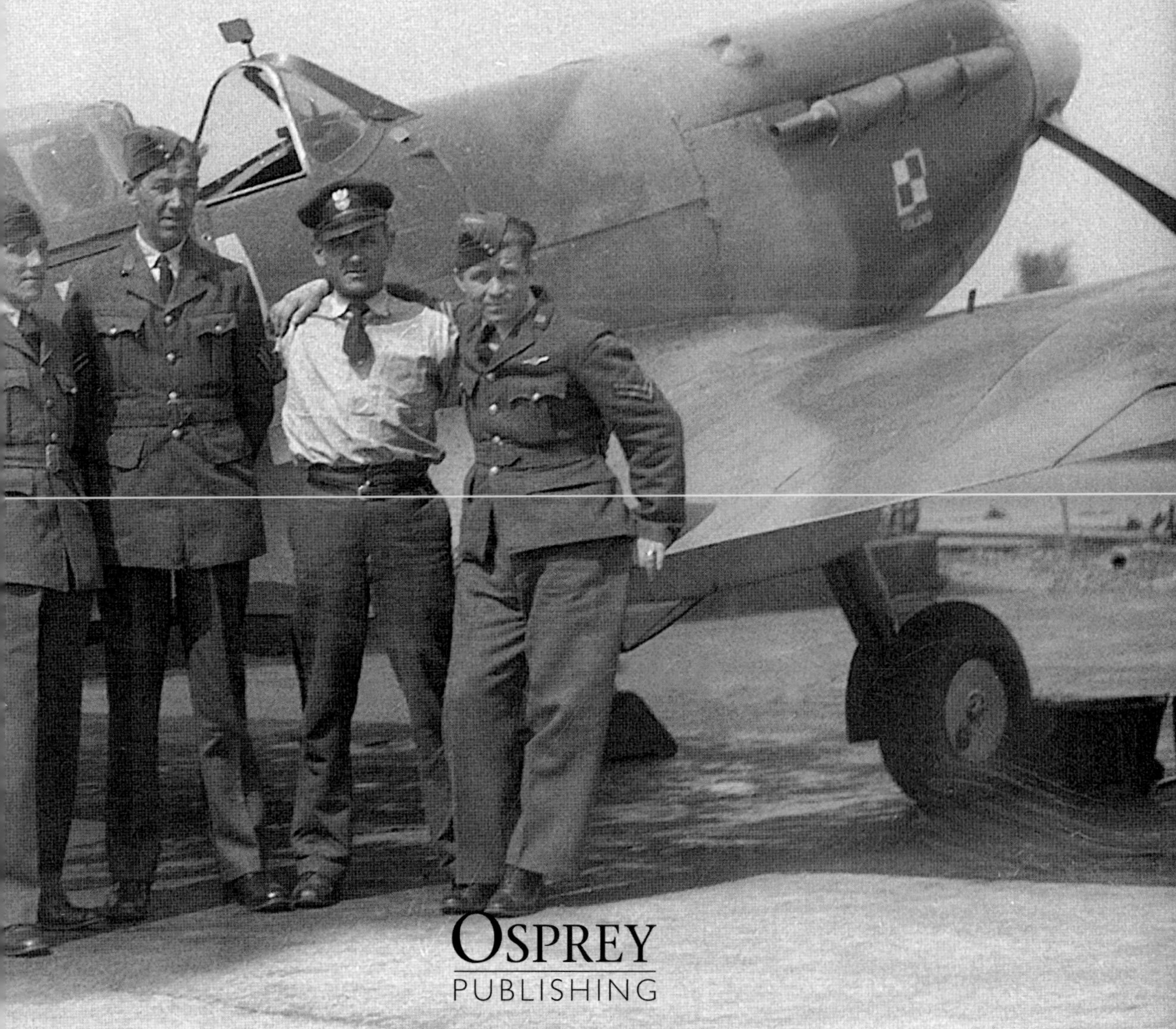

OSPREY PUBLISHING

First published in Great Britain in 2015 by Osprey Publishing
PO Box 883, Oxford, OX1 9PL, UK
PO Box 3985, New York, NY 10185–3985, USA

E-mail: info@ospreypublishing.com

Osprey Publishing, part of Bloomsbury Publishing Plc

A CIP catalogue record for this book is available from the British Library

ISBN: 978 1 4728 0837 0
PDF e-book ISBN: 978 1 4728 0838 7
e-Pub ISBN: 978 1 4728 0839 4

Edited by Tony Holmes and Philip Jarrett
Cover Artwork by Mark Postlethwaite
Aircraft Profiles by Robert Grudzień
Index by Sandra Shotter
Originated by PDQ Digital Media Solutions, UK
Printed in China through World Print Limited

15 16 17 18 19 10 9 8 7 6 5 4 3 2 1

Osprey Publishing is supporting the Woodland Trust, the UK's leading woodland conservation charity, by funding the dedication of trees.

www.ospreypublishing.com

Acknowledgements
I would like to thank fellow researchers and friends who assisted me with valuable information and illustrations – Peter Arnold, Mark Baczkiewicz, the Benz family, Mark Crame, Jerzy B Cynk, Tomasz Drecki, Robert Gretzyngier, Robert Grudzień, Adam Jackowski, Tomasz Kopański, Krzysztof Kubala, Zbigniew Legierski, Krzysztof Mroczkowski, Lechosław Musiałkowski, Dr Alfred Price, Wojciech Sankowski, Andy Saunders, Piotr Sikora, Grzegorz Sojda, Robert Stachyra, Grzegorz Śliżewski, Helmut Terbeck, Andy Thomas, Paweł Tuliński, Ryszard Witkowski and Józef Zieliński. Special thanks to Bob Sikkel and Wojciech Zmyślony for their invaluable input.

Front Cover
The summer of 1943 saw squadrons of the Northolt-based 1st Polish Wing repeatedly engaged in 'Ramrod' operations, escorting USAAF bombers to targets on the European Continent. Wg Cdr Aleksander Gabszewicz, the Northolt Wing Leader, said in his report from the morning operation on 19 August;

'As the Wing Leader I was leading 316 (Polish) Squadron, which was the leading Squadron in the Wing taking part in Ramrod 209, with the task of providing forward target support for 36 Marauders bombing Amiens/Glissy aerodrome. Wing took off at 1035 hrs and made straight for France. When approaching Amiens I got a warning from Operations of e/a [enemy aircraft] north of Amiens. At the same time the leader of "A" Flight, Flt Lt Jeka, saw some Huns nearby and went to attack them. I then gave the order for the whole Squadron to attack.'

Józef Jeka subsequently reported the ensuing engagement;

'I was the leader of the port section of four aircraft in Ramrod 209 over Amiens. Flying at about 26,000 ft, I saw a number of Fw 190s (15 to 20) below me in front to the left. Attacking with my section, I noticed a single Fw 190 to the left of me. As it was much nearer to me I turned left and opened fire at an angle of 30 to 40 degrees from a distance of 150 yards down to 80 yards. I observed bullets entering the e/a at the pilot's cockpit and wings. Being afraid of a collision I broke off the combat, and as I pulled up I completely blacked out for a few seconds, and therefore could not observe any more. However, two pilots from my section, Flg Off Wiza and WO Gallus, reported that they saw large pieces falling off the aircraft, which then went down in a half-spin/half-spiral, trailing smoke behind it. A few seconds later it burst into flames. Owing to the report from these two pilots I claim this aircraft as destroyed.

'After recovering from the blackout I saw another Fw 190 about 2000 ft below me to the right. I immediately attacked it from behind and seven to ten degrees to the right, and with the advantage of height. Closing the range to about 100-150 yards, I gave the Hun a short burst, observing strikes in the cockpit and fuselage. It was a successful surprise attack. The Hun rolled over and I pressed the button again, but my cannon did not fire – stoppage. I broke off as I saw some more Huns coming nearer. I tested the cannon and guns a few times, but the stoppage in both cannon prevented me from firing them. This aircraft I claim as damaged.'

Overall, the 1st Polish Wing was credited with six Fw 190s destroyed, one probable and three damaged, Gabszewicz and Jeka each claiming one destroyed and one damaged. These proved to be the final victories against manned aircraft for both aces, although Jeka subsequently destroyed one of the last V1 flying bombs credited to Polish pilots (flying a No 306 Sqn Mustang III) in March 1945 (*Cover artwork by Mark Postlethwaite*)

CONTENTS

The Polish-designed and -built PZL P.24 fighter, first flown in early 1934, outperformed all of the contenders to Specification F.7/30 for a day and nightfighter, including the Supermarine Type 224. The P.24 was briefly considered for the RAF, but 'the question of policy of adopting a Polish-designed aircraft' must have raised some eyebrows at the Air Ministry. RAF fighter squadrons re-equipped with the Gloster Gladiator instead of the Polish cannon-armed P.24, and R J Mitchell kept on working on his fighter, eventually creating the Spitfire

INTRODUCTION

GET THE SPITFIRE

The Polish connection with the Spitfire started long before World War 2. In fact, it might have ended the story of the Supermarine fighter before it had even started! A memo for the Deputy Chief of Air Staff (DCAS), Air Vice-Marshal M Edgar Ludlow-Hewitt, dated 25 April 1934, said;

'Further information is now available about the Polish P.Z.24 fighter, which you will remember Sir John Higgins [the previous Air Member for Supply & Research (AMSR)] wanted the Air Ministry to buy to compete with the F.7/30 day and nightfighters which are due shortly at Martlesham.

'P.Z.24 in comparison with predicted performance of F.7/30 Supermarines. (It should be noted that we have no test figures for the Supermarine as yet. On paper it is the fastest of the F.7/30 class now building.)

'(i) P.Z.24 is 4 mph faster than the Supermarine and climbs to 15,000 ft in 2½ minutes less.

'(ii) On the other hand, the P.Z.24 has two guns and 600 rounds of ammunition against four guns and 2000 rounds of ammunition.

'AMSR [Air Marshal Hugh Dowding] and DTD [Directorate of Technical Development] are both opposed to the P.Z.24 being tried out in the day and nightfighter category, but AMSR suggests that it might be of interest as an interceptor ([Hawker] Fury replacement), for which we are issuing a specification this year.

'Quite apart from the question of policy of adopting a Polish-designed aircraft to meet our own fighter requirements, I think that the P.Z.24 will be out of date by the time we get the Fury replacement [please, note that throughout this book the vocabulary and grammar of quoted documents has been updated for easier reading in line with *Osprey Aircraft of the Aces* series style].'

With hindsight, the data quoted in the document was inaccurate. The Polish fighter's correct designation was PZL P.24. Its top speed was 258 mph, some 20 mph (rather than 4 mph) more than what the Supermarine Type 224 (F.7/30) ever attained. Also, the production P.24 was the world's first series-built fighter with twin wing-mounted 20 mm cannon, rather than just two machine guns.

All in all, had the DCAS known the true data, and had he decided to ignore the 'question of policy of adopting a Polish-designed aircraft', history might have been very different. Had the PZL P.24 been ordered for RAF squadrons, the Supermarine Type 224 fighter might have been the principal victim. As it actually happened, the PZL offer was rejected and the Gloster Gladiator ordered as a stopgap in face of the failure of all original F.7/30 contenders. The later Spitfire, which was a new design and only tenuously related to the Supermarine Type 224 tendered to the F.7/30 specification, emerged as one of the 'Fury replacements'.

Such was the pace of aircraft development at the time that merely five years later, in 1939, it was Poland's turn to drop the policy of buying only Polish-designed and -built combat aircraft. In June 1939 a Polish Military Mission was sent to Britain to negotiate the purchase of military equipment. A contract was eventually signed for the delivery of 14 Hawker Hurricanes (as well as bombers and other equipment). At the time the Polish Air Force (PAF) was equipped mostly with all-metal aircraft of monocoque design,

Lt Col Jerzy Bajan was a famous PAF pilot before World War 2, participating in numerous air races and competitions. He had also originated Poland's first aerobatic team, the 'Bajan Trio', two members of which, Kazimierz Kosiński and Karol Pniak, achieved acedom in World War 2. Bajan was appointed Commandant of the PAF College at Dęblin in June 1939. Soon afterwards he was one of four Polish pilots who test-flew the Spitfire in Britain. Wounded during the German bombing of Dęblin at the outbreak of the war, his left hand never recovered. Reaching Britain with other Polish servicemen, he trained on Spitfires despite his disability, and flew a tour of operations with No 316 Sqn to gain first-hand experience of modern fighter tactics. Following the death of Gp Capt Pawlikowski, he was appointed Senior Polish Liaison Officer to HQ Fighter Command, or the head of the exiled Polish fighter force. At the end of the war he presided over the PAF committee that produced an official listing of individual pilots' scores, known to historians as the 'Bajan List', which was the primary source for score data quoted in this book (see Appendix 1 for more details)

and in this respect the Hurricane was a step backwards. Lt Col Bogdan Kwieciński, the Military and Air Attaché at the Polish Embassy in London, explained in his report to Poland, 'As regards Spitfires, I should stress that we make efforts to get at least one example for test purposes, since this type is better suited for possible manufacture in our country'. Soon he was able to report 'the Air Ministry has allocated one Spitfire aircraft for us'.

Meanwhile, a team of Polish test pilots – Jerzy Bajan, Andrzej Włodarkiewicz, Roland Kalpas and Bolesław Orliński – went to Britain in June 1939. They flew new aircraft types, including the Spitfire. Eventually, the sole Spitfire sold to Poland, L1066, was despatched (on the MV *Lassell*, together with Hurricanes and Fairey Battles) only after the German invasion of the country on 1 September 1939. Faced with the collapse of Polish resistance after the Soviet invasion, the British government offered the entire shipment to Turkey on 17 September. Consequently, L1066 was delivered as part of that country's order for Spitfire Is. It was allocated to the 42. *Av Bölük* (42nd Fighter Company) of the VIII. *Av Taburu* (8th Fighter Battalion) of the 4ncü *Hava Alay* (4th Air Regiment), based at Corlu, near Istanbul. At that time the unit was equipped with PZL P.24s (and was about to convert onto Hurricanes).

By the end of 1940 all three Turkish Spitfire Is (P9566 and P9567 were delivered in 1940) had been grounded owing to a lack of spares, and by April 1942 at least two of them had found their way to the RAF in Egypt. Their original serial numbers being unknown, they were given new ones – HK854 and HK856 (HK857 in the same block has not been linked to any aircraft so far) – in a block allocated to impressed aircraft. So perhaps the ex-Polish Spitfire I was eventually used by the RAF in the Middle East.

To return to the four Polish test pilots in the summer of 1939, it is not certain which Spitfire I they flew. Most probably it was K9791, as this aeroplane was provided for similar flights to other visitors. By a strange twist of fate, K9791 was almost certainly the first Spitfire to be shown to the Polish public – but not in pleasant circumstances. Shot down on 17 August 1940 over the Continent, it was put on show in various parts of German-occupied Europe as a war prize, including the city of Cracow, in Poland, in July 1942.

CHAPTER ONE

DEFENDING BRITAIN

Jeffrey Quill, the iconic Supermarine test pilot, referred to 'YT-J, the squadron aircraft allotted to me' when identifying the Spitfire he flew with No 65 Sqn during the Battle of Britain in order to obtain first-hand data on the type's performance in combat. He left the unit at the end of August, and some ten weeks later his former Spitfire became the usual mount of Polish ace-to-be Plt Off Bolesław Drobiński. Note the *EAST INDIA FUND FLIGHT* inscription stencilled on this side of the fuselage

Although the Luftwaffe later claimed to have destroyed the PAF on the ground on 1 September 1939, this was a lie. Polish squadrons had moved to camouflaged forward airfields at the end of August, when the German attack was imminent. In the first days of the war Polish air defence did reasonably well, considering the overall situation, but soon there were many more skilled pilots than serviceable aircraft. The German *Blitzkrieg* (lightning war) stretched Polish communications and logistics beyond their capacity (as it would against the British and French nine months later). Many repairable aircraft were lost through lack of spares or facilities, and sometimes owing to a lack of fuel. Poor aircraft recognition among the ground forces led to numerous 'friendly fire' incidents.

When France and Britain declared war on Germany on 3 September it was hoped that the conflict would soon be won. However, when the Soviet Union opened the second front, invading Poland on 17 September and effectively stabbing the Polish defensive lines in the back, further armed resistance became impossible. However, there was never an overall surrender of Polish forces, and it was obvious to the Poles that they would continue fighting in any theatre of operations they could.

Most PAF personnel evaded capture and went to neutral Rumania and Hungary, Poland's southern neighbours at the time, and thence to France. No fewer than 8500 PAF servicemen had arrived there by April 1940. In a few weeks the Polish government re-formed in exile in France, and the re-establishment of Polish armed forces started there. While it was obvious that the Polish Army would reorganise and operate on French soil, the Poles originally preferred to have their air force re-formed in Britain, as British technology and organisation were held in higher esteem. However, at the time Britain was observing a policy of 'no foreign forces on our soil'. Polish authorities were therefore notified that air units could be formed of Polish personnel only as part of the RAF, and all their members would have to swear allegiance to the British monarch. This soon resulted in the first crisis. A group of Polish servicemen (including future aces Stanisław Blok and Grzegorz Sołogub) refused to pledge loyalty to the king and were sent back to France.

Moreover, only Polish bomber units could be formed in Britain. Apparently, with Fighter Command's sophisticated ground control system, spoken English was a prerequisite for any fighter pilot to fly on operations, and very few Poles spoke any English at all (at the time it was not the worldwide *lingua franca* that it is today). There was no such requirement for bomber crews – they were expected to take off, find their target, bomb it and, hopefully, return, regardless of the language they spoke.

In late 1939 the Poles were regarded by their two Western allies as survivors of a pathetically weak country, overrun by the Germans and Soviets within a few weeks. All that the Polish authorities-in-exile could do was accept the harsh terms dictated by what were considered to be the world's two greatest powers. So volunteers for Polish bomber squadrons started coming from France to England. Surprisingly, some of the top Polish fighter pilots, including men such as Stanisław Skalski, Karol Pniak and Henryk Szczęsny, who already had multiple aerial victories to their credit over Poland, chose to come to Britain, even if it meant they would now fly bombers and act as half-mercenaries for a foreign realm.

Meanwhile, several Polish fighter squadrons started to be formed in France, and one of them was ready for action by the time the fighting began in earnest in May 1940. The other Polish squadrons-to-be were bled away when their air- and groundcrews were posted in sections to French units.

Then, when the French campaign suddenly ended after a few weeks, the Poles' situation changed significantly. France had collapsed in about as much time as Poland, despite the former's significantly greater military power. The British Expeditionary Forces had achieved only one 'success' in the Battle of France – the evacuation of Dunkirk. By the end of June 1940 Britain was left alone to face what seemed to be an imminent German invasion. Overnight, the Poles, so far unimportant troops from a far away defeated country, turned into the sole staunch ally of the British Empire. His Majesty's Government now proved willing to accept far reaching concessions, and Parliament wasted no time in passing a new law that allowed armed forces of Allied countries to be based on British soil after all. On 5 August a Polish-British agreement was signed to form Polish Armed Forces in Britain. It stated;

'Polish Armed Forces (comprising Land, Sea and Air Forces) shall be organised and employed, under British Command in its character as the Allied High Command, as the Armed Forces of the Republic of Poland allied with the United Kingdom. The personnel of the Polish Air Force will take an oath of allegiance to the Polish Republic.'

The PAF Inspectorate General (later re-formed into PAF HQ) was based in London. Polish units were integrated with the RAF operational structure, so for the duration of the war the Inspectorate (HQ) had only indirect operational control of Polish squadrons. Rather than exercise command of the entire Polish fighter and bomber forces, Polish liaison officers were posted to RAF HQs at various levels. Importantly, the Polish-British agreements introduced a rather complicated system of double ranks for Polish personnel. The Polish and British ranks of an individual did not have to be equal (and often were not). For practical reasons the British ranks were important for operational personnel, as these defined what they were to be paid. Throughout the hostilities all costs relating to the operation of Polish forces were credited by HM Government, to be paid after the war (which they eventually were).

Another thing agreed quite early on was that aircraft of the Polish (and subsequently other exiled) units would be marked with standard RAF roundels and fin flashes, with only small national markings. This was to avoid confusion of varying insignia in combat situations. Following the same thinking, RAF and Fleet Air Arm aircraft adopted US star markings during the Operation *Torch* landings in North Africa in November 1942. It is easy to imagine that the Polish white-and-red 'checks', square-shaped and with distinctive angular features, could be much more easily confused with the German crosses than the circular British roundels.

Ten Polish squadrons were formed in 1940, including four day fighter units, followed by three more day fighter squadrons in early 1941. Until the end of World War 2, the PAF was by far the largest exiled air force of any occupied nation. One particular feature that distinguished the Poles from other exiled air forces was that both air- and groundcrews were Polish. In the squadrons of other exiled nations formed alongside the RAF, the ground personnel were usually entirely or mostly British. Also unmatched by virtually all exiled air forces was the scope of training and auxiliary services formed by the PAF in Britain to support the operational units. A number of schools for air- and groundcrew trades were created, ranging from initial training establishments up to a staff college. Last, but certainly not least, numerous Polish girls joined the Polish Womens' Auxiliary Air Force (WAAF) branch.

Of course, during the summer of 1940 this 'big picture' was only being sketched out by British and Polish high commands. What mattered most for both nations at the time was to defend Britain, and thus ensure that Hitler (and his Soviet ally) was not given free rein throughout Europe.

BATTLE OF BRITAIN

On the eve of the Battle of Britain there were two main groups of PAF pilots in the British Isles – those who had come in late 1939 and early 1940 to man the bomber squadrons and those who had been evacuated from France only when it surrendered. The former group had spent months learning English and the King's Regulations, but doing little flying. Many of the latter had been flying in France until the end (operationally or in training) but spoke no English and knew nothing about the King or his regulations!

On 5 December 1940 Henryk 'Sneezy' Szczęsny became the first Polish Spitfire ace when he achieved his fifth victory on the type with No 74 Sqn. This photograph was taken about a year later, when he was CO of No 317 Sqn, but he still had No 74 Sqn's 'Tiger' motif on his Mae West

With Fighter Command in dire need of reinforcements, these two groups of Poles were employed in two different ways. Those already well versed in British procedures and local language were hurriedly subjected to refresher flying and operational training, then posted to RAF squadrons. The recent arrivals were to form PAF units, needing to learn only basic commands in English. Notably, while Polish bomber squadrons were just given RAF liaison officers or assistants, Fighter Command insisted on full dual command, with both squadron and flight commanders being British, doubled by their Polish opposite numbers. This procedure was followed until early 1941. This sometimes led to situations that seem amusing now, but could be embarrassing or annoying at the time. For example, when No 303 Sqn was originally formed at Northolt in 1940, the only pilot with no experience whatsoever in fighters was one of its British flight commanders.

Six Polish pilots were already aces when they arrived in Britain – Sqn Ldr Mieczysław Mümler, Plt Offs Czesław Główczyński, Władysław Gnyś and Stanisław Skalski and Sgts Jan Kremski and Eugeniusz Nowakiewicz. All would fly Spitfires from 1941 onwards. Skalski had qualified as an ace over Poland in 1939, Nowakiewicz scored all of his victories over France in early 1940 and the others had 'mixed bags' from both campaigns. Sixteen more Polish pilots were to become aces during the Battle of Britain, but only one of them on Spitfires. Of the 15 Hurricane aces, nine flew with No 303 Sqn and one with No 302 Sqn. Two Polish aces were killed before the end of the Battle, but the rest later flew Spitfires, and in most cases added to their scores in them.

Since all Polish fighter squadrons were initially equipped with Hurricanes, the first Polish Spitfire aces were among those posted to RAF units. As mentioned earlier, Flg Off Henryk Szczęsny had several victories from the Polish campaign to his credit when he arrived in Britain in February 1940. Posted to No 74 Sqn at Hornchurch on 5 August, he was nicknamed 'Sneezy' by his commonwealth colleagues, who were unable to pronounce his name correctly. He scored his first Spitfire kill on 13 August at about 0700 hrs, describing the action in his combat report;

'I saw three [Dornier] Do 17s in front of me. I went to attack No 3 of the formation when he swung round to the right. I broke away to the left and came round behind the Dos onto their tails. One of the machines was out of formation and I attacked it from astern. At this point the Do dropped several bombs in the sea. I got a good burst in from very close range and the Do started to dive towards the sea. He tried to land there, but as he flattened out he burst into flames and toppled straight into the water. This must have been somewhere in the Estuary east of the Isle of

Sheppey. I did not know where I was and managed to force-land at Maidstone with my undercarriage up, as I could not get it down.'

This was the first Spitfire victory credited to any Polish ace, with Szczęsny flying Spitfire I K9871/ZP-O on this occasion. Some nine hours later another Pole opened his Spitfire score, this time flying from Middle Wallop with No 609 Sqn. In his report, Flg Off Tadeusz Nowierski, nicknamed 'Novi' by his British friends, wrote;

'I was Green 2, and we sighted a large number of enemy aircraft coming from the South. We circled above them, and Green 1 dived to attack. At that moment I saw one Me 109 [i.e. Bf 109] above me and ahead. I climbed up behind him and fired three bursts at fairly close range and dead astern. White smoke appeared from his fuselage and he turned over and started to dive. Some large object, probably the cockpit door or roof, flew away and the pilot got out and opened his parachute. I then saw two Me 109s behind me and I dived and pulled out in a violent left hand turn and "blacked out". Ten minutes later I saw another Me 109 ahead and approached him from behind and gave him a good burst at very close range. White smoke appeared from the fuselage and he dived steeply into a cloud and disappeared. I dived through the cloud and a minute or so later saw another aircraft dive into the sea. This occurred too late for it to be my victim. Before attacking my first Me 109 I saw a Spitfire attack and shoot down an Me 109. This was probably Plt Off Crook.'

All references to victory claims and credits cited in this book use aircraft type designations as included in relevant documents of the period. In particular, this applies to the 'Me 109', as that is how the Messerschmitt Bf 109 was described in contemporary combat reports.

Nowierski was credited with a 'Me 109' destroyed and another damaged following this combat, flying Spitfire I L1082/PR-A. As far as can be ascertained, this was the first fighter combat of his career. Unlike virtually all of his fellow aces, he had been a reconnaissance bomber pilot from 1929 through to the 1939 campaign. On 15 August Nowierski had an inconclusive combat, describing it as follows;

'I was Blue 2 Leader, manoeuvring into position to attack. As we turned to attack I saw on my right at the same height five enemy aircraft coming towards me. I turned towards them – they were [Junkers] Ju 88s – and as we passed them I turned to attack. Just as I got within range they turned into the sun right across my path and I got in a one second burst on the second aircraft before having to break off very quickly. I flick rolled and blacked out, and by the time I came to I had lost sight of the enemy. I climbed up again to approximately 10,000 ft and saw one enemy aircraft going in a southerly direction. I climbed above him into the sun. I attacked and gave him a burst from the rear quarter. He turned into the sun and I followed, overtaking very fast in lead line astern. I throttled back so as not to overtake him. Although I could not see well because of the sun, I opened fire, but then I had

A seemingly anonymous Spitfire II in Battle of Britain-period markings on a 'Queen Mary' trailer. The little PAF red-and-white square under the windscreen suggests the usual pilot's nationality. No Polish units converted to the type before Sky replaced black as the spinner colour, so this aircraft must have come from an RAF squadron. The most probable candidate is P7361, flown regularly by Flg Off Szczęsny with No 74 Sqn (*via Andy Saunders*)

to throttle back and he drew away. I had no more ammunition so I went back to base.'

This account provides a good example of the general confusion typical of the rapid encounters between fast, manoeuvring aircraft. Notably, on that occasion, Nowierski was flying Spitfire I R6915/PR-O, which survives today in the Imperial War Museum collection.

Szczęsny became the first Polish Spitfire ace when he achieved his fifth victory in the aeroplane on 5 December 1940. At the time his total score was seven and one shared confirmed destroyed, one probable and two damaged.

'Novi' was credited with five and one shared destroyed and two damaged enemy aircraft in the 'Report on Polish Pilots' made by Sqn Ldr Michael Robinson, Officer Commanding No 609 Sqn, on 8 February 1941. For obscure reasons several of these victories were subsequently downgraded from 'destroyed' to 'damaged' in the official PAF victory listing.

According to RAF documents, Tadeusz 'Novi' Nowierski was the next Polish pilot credited with five confirmed victories on Spitfires, having scored them during his time with No 609 Sqn (August 1940 to February 1941). Oddly, the official PAF scoreboard at war's end credited him with just three kills during this period

Apart from 'Novi' and 'Sneezy', only one other future Polish ace flew Spitfires in the Battle of Britain – Bolesław Drobiński. Posted to No 65 Sqn in August, he continued to fly with the unit until early 1941, but failed to achieve any success. However, he clearly gained enough experience on the fighter to become one of the leading Spitfire scorers during the summer of 1941.

Many Polish Hurricane pilots of the Battle later claimed victories with the Spitfire. Flg Off Marian Pisarek, Plt Offs Stanisław Skalski, Jerzy Popławski and Jan Zumbach and Sgt Michał Maciejowski all claimed victories with Hurricane squadrons during the Battle, and were later credited with five or more kills in Spitfires as well. Plt Offs Mirosław Ferić and Witold Łokuciewski and Sgts Antoni Głowacki and Józef Jeka achieved 'acedom' in the Hurricane during the Battle, and subsequently flew Spitfires, scoring less than five kills with the latter. Other aces who scored in Hurricanes in 1940 and with Spitfires later on included Flg Offs Tadeusz Nowak and Wacław Łapkowski, Plt Offs Wacław Król and Jerzy Radomski and Sgts Marian Bełc, Mirosław Wojciechowski and Kazimierz Wünsche.

Air defence of the British Isles against intensive German bombing raids did not end on 31 October, although this date is nowadays recognised as the last day of the Battle of Britain. German bombers gradually switched to night attacks, and continued to conduct heavy raids against British cities until May 1941. By then Fighter Command was already on the offensive, however.

Plt Off Bolesław Drobiński was the top-scoring Polish pilot on Spitfire IIBs, claiming six confirmed and a shared probable with the variant. He later added to his score flying Spitfire Vs

CHAPTER TWO

HOT SUMMER OF 1941

By April 1941 the PAF in Britain had seven day fighter units – Nos 302, 303, 306, 308, 315, 316 and 317 Sqns. In line with the Fighter Command reshaping, which called for combined operational use of multiple squadron formations, two Polish wings were formed during the spring/summer of 1941. Moving from defence to offence, the 1st Polish Wing at Northolt participated in the most intensive daylight operations over occupied France and Belgium. The 2nd Polish Wing (initially with headquarters at Exeter) flew patrols off the southwest British coast and carried out some offensive operations. Because of uneven combat pressure on the two wings, squadrons rotated. Following several months of intensive combat flying from Northolt they moved elsewhere for rest and replenishment.

To facilitate training of single-seat fighter pilots for Polish squadrons, the Polish Fighter School (*Polska Szkoła Myśliwska*, or PSM) was formed in the spring of 1941. Although regarded as a separate establishment by the PAF, it was integrated with RAF Operational Training Units (OTUs). Initially it operated within No 55 OTU, equipped with Hurricanes. In the summer of 1941 a parallel course on Spitfires was started at No 61 OTU at Heston. Eventually, in late 1941, the two sections of the PSM merged within No 58 OTU at Grangemouth, and then trained all Polish fighter pilots (solely on Spitfires) until 1943. In October 1943 that OTU re-formed into No 2 Tactical Exercise Unit and the Polish school was transferred to No 61 OTU at Rednal, where it continued to exist until the end of the war. Tour-expired pilots, including most of the aces mentioned in this book, were periodically posted to the OTUs as instructors so that they could pass on their know-how to less experienced colleagues.

FIRST POLISH SPITFIRE SQUADRONS

The first Polish unit to convert to Spitfires was No 303 Sqn, which received Mk Is in late January 1941. These were replaced by Mk IIAs in March, and then by Mk IIBs in May. The next unit to switch from Hurricanes to Spitfires was No 308 Sqn, which received its Mk Is in April and Mk IIs in May. Thus, when Fighter Command's 'non-stop offensive' commenced, the PAF had two Spitfire squadrons. By the end of June No 308 Sqn had joined No 303 Sqn at Northolt, together with No 306 Sqn, then in the process of replacing its Hurricane IIAs and IIBs with Spitfire IIBs.

The Combat Diary of RAF Station Northolt summed June 1941 up in the following way;

'Fighter sweeps occupied the first half of the month, and upon Germany threatening Russia the Circus activity over France was increased. The date of the change may be accepted as 16 June. Between then and the end of the month 15 Circus operations took place – up to that time only 12 had ever taken place. This increase in activity brought No 308 Sqn – a new Polish squadron – into the frontline, and the days were reminiscent of the "Battle of Britain".'

Whenever weather permitted, July and August followed the intensive operational flying pattern of late June. The 'Circus' codename for the operations was not really a code. The actual primary objective of these missions was not to hit any ground targets with bombs, but to draw enemy fighters into battle by staging a 'show' that was convincing enough. If the objective was really to destroy the target by bombing, the operation was codenamed 'Ramrod', but such missions were scarce at the time. The August 1941 summary of the RAF Northolt Combat Diary was surprisingly honest about how effective the bombing was during the majority of these operations;

'The bombing on the whole was inaccurate, although some efforts were very good.'

The standard pattern of 'Circus' operations was, therefore, to wait for German fighters to attack the bombers or escort, then engage them. A typical personal combat report (PCR) from that period described the victory of Sgt Marian Bełc of No 303 Sqn, flying Spitfire IIB P8531/RF-Y, during 'Circus 21' on 24 June 1941;

'I was flying with Sqn Ldr Łapkowski, who was leading No 303 Sqn as top escort to the bombers. We had been

This aircraft, R6975/RF-A, was one of first Spitfire Is delivered to No 303 Sqn in January 1941. It became the usual mount of ace Sqn Ldr Zdzisław Henneberg. Note the Sky spinner and black underside of the port wing – quick-recognition markings introduced by Fighter Command in late 1940. The black wing was abandoned in April 1941 when German fighters became scarce over Britain

'Tolo' Łokuciewski was the first ace to score a Spitfire victory with a Polish squadron. He did so during a 'Sphere' operation on 20 April 1941 in a No 303 Sqn Mk IIA. This photograph was taken in late 1941 or early 1942, by which time Łokuciewski was No 303 Sqn's 'A' Flight commander

During May 1941 No 303 Sqn converted to the cannon-armed Spitfire IIB, with which it then participated in Fighter Command's 'non-stop offensive' until mid-July. This machine, P8507/RF-V, was the personal mount of squadron commander, Sqn Ldr Wacław Łapkowski, who scored four confirmed kills in it during June. The group here includes two future Spitfire aces, namely Bolesław Gładych (standing far right) and Bolesław Drobiński (standing far left)

watching for the Me 109s to starboard and above us. Near the coast one pair dived down to attack the bombers, and they were in turn attacked by Sqn Ldr Łapkowski. The second pair then dived to attack the bombers and I went after them, getting in a short burst at the leader, who broke off and dived away. The second one stayed in a climbing turn to port. I pulled up my nose and gave a short burst with cannon and machine gun from 120/100yds. I saw the whole of the Me 109F's tail unit break off, and the enemy aircraft turned on its back and went down like a stone from 7000 ft.'

This was the fifth kill credited to Bełc, but his first with a Spitfire. He had earlier claimed an 'Me 109' destroyed over Poland in a PZL P.11 with the 152nd *Eskadra*, and then two 'Me 109s' and an 'Me 110' with No 303 Sqn during the Battle of Britain. In the same operation Łapkowski, flying his lucky Spitfire IIB P8507/RF-V, was credited with his seventh confirmed victory (his fourth with the Spitfire). This also proved to be his last, for at the end of June he chose a new RF-V (Mk IIB P8596) and was duly shot down and killed in it during 'Circus 29' on 2 July.

Another ace, Plt Off Bolesław Drobiński, also scored most of his kills in just one Spitfire IIB. This is his report from 'Circus 22' on 25 June, when he scored his fifth confirmed victory;

'I left the squadron formation to follow two Me 109Fs that were diving down. I got in a short burst at one of them from 300/400 yards, but he half-rolled and I missed him. I fired again from 250 yards with cannon and machine gun, and the Me 109F half-rolled a second time and went straight down. I was not quite sure whether he was finished or not, and as it went down I put in a third burst, and it went into the ground 5-7 miles East of Gravelines. This combat started at 12,000 ft and finished at 1000 ft.'

Drobiński had gained his first aerial victory just a week before, during 'Circus 15' on 18 June. All five were scored in Spitfire IIB P8335/RF-R. This was the top-scoring Spitfire (of any mark) in the hands of Polish pilots. Although Plt Off Władysław Drecki claimed two more 'Me 109s' destroyed in it during 'Circus 26' on 28 June, he had to ditch the aircraft in the Channel after the lengthy combat, which had cost him too much fuel. Drobiński then continued to fly other RF-R-coded Spitfires, and his entire further score was achieved in these – Mk IIB P8461 on 3 and 6 July 1941 and Mk VB AB929 on 24 October 1941 and 13 March 1942.

Aerial encounters were not the only opportunity to engage the Luftwaffe. Attacks were also made against German installations on the ground in occupied Europe. Missions flown by small groups of fighters against ground targets were initially codenamed 'Mosquito', then 'Sphere' and finally 'Rhubarb'. Enemy airfields were targeted whenever possible. Future ace Flt Lt Stefan Janus opened his score with

No 308 Sqn during 'Circus 58' on 22 July, flying Spitfire IIB P8326/ZF-F. He reported;

'Near Guines we attacked an aerodrome. I fired at ground defence posts and hangars, after passing the hangars I saw two Me 109Es hidden among the trees – I fired at them with my cannon, seeing pieces flying from them, and as I passed over them I saw they were both in flames. As we crossed the Coast I heard Plt Off Bożek asking for Air/Sea Rescue [ASR]. I turned back, and saw three Me 109s attacking one Spitfire with the letter "E" (Plt Off Kremski). One of them was diving on the Spitfire from astern. As I approached on the starboard side of the Spitfire, the enemy aircraft banked over to the left and started to climb away, presenting me with a perfect plan view at a range of 100 yards. I gave him a short burst from all my guns – I saw thick smoke come from the engine. I turned and lost sight of him for a moment, and on completing my turn saw the Me 109, with clouds of black smoke pouring from it, plunge into the Channel.'

Two Battle of Britain aces and friends from No 303 Sqn, in which they were both flight commanders – Pole Marian Pisarek (left) and Canadian Johnny Kent. By the time this photograph was taken, in the summer of 1941, Kent was the leader of the Polish Northolt Wing and Pisarek commanded No 308 Sqn within the wing

Sadly, the ASR failed to locate Plt Off Władysław Bożek, who perished in the Channel. Jan Kremski, on the other hand, scored his final (ninth) victory during this operation. This was his second on Spitfires. Rather unusually among Polish aces, Kremski had scored most of his victories before arriving in Britain – one and two shared over Poland in 1939, followed by four shared over France in May and June 1940. Kremski was then shot down and killed during 'Circus 73' on 14 August 1941, flying the same 'Spitfire with the letter "E"' (Mk IIB P8310/ZF-E) that Janus mentions in the report above.

The Luftwaffe was not the only threat to fighter pilots, however. During 'Circus 61' on 24 July, No 308 Sqn lost two pilots to German fighters (Plt Off Józef Czachowski, 'on loan' from No 315 Sqn, was killed, and Flg Off

Spitfire IIB P8385/RF-A was a presentation aircraft funded by employees of the Rushden and Higham Ferrers Boot and Shoe Company and named *IMPREGNABLE*. It sported an image of Disney character 'Goofy the Dog' watching a German aircraft trailing smoke. Here, Flg Off Bronisław Kłosin is posing with the aircraft, even though the Spitfire was usually flown by ace Flg Off Mirosław Ferić. Indeed, he was credited with a confirmed victory in it during 'Circus 18' on 22 June. P8385 was also occasionally flown by other pilots, and ace Flg Off Jan Zumbach scored a confirmed kill and a probable in it during 'Circus 29' on 2 July

Władysław Chciuk became a PoW) and came close to losing two more in an aerial collision when Plt Off Jan Jakubowski collided with squadron commander Sqn Ldr Marian Pisarek. The latter's Spitfire IIB, P8676/ZF-H, lost a large part of its port wing, but the ace managed to bring the fighter back to Northolt. His landing of the crippled fighter was witnessed by a man in the neighbourhood, who then wrote the following letter to RAF Station Northolt;

'Dear Sir,

'As an ex-Royal Flying Corps Boy I cannot let the most wonderful exhibition of flying that I have ever had the honour to see pass without expressing my admiration for the pilot, who was flying the Spitfire which I saw coming home about 3.45 pm yesterday with nearly half of his left wing shot away. The manner in which that machine was handled was magnificent, and the pilot, whoever he is, for exhibiting such grandeur in the air, must be a sure candidate for some distinguished flying honour.

'The Very Best of Luck to Him and all the other grand Boys who are doing their stuff.

'Yours faithfully
'F R Brown.'

QUALITIES OF POLISH FIGHTER PILOTS

It was at about this time that Gp Capt Theodore McEvoy, the Station Commander at RAF Northolt, also expressed his opinion of the quality of Polish fighter pilots in an official report. It is quoted here in its entirety, as the report contradicts some popular clichés, as well as confirming some others;

'SECRET
'THE POLISH FIGHTER PILOT
'After only four months as the Commander of a Station of three Polish Fighter Squadrons it would be presumptuous to essay an analysis of the character and qualities of Polish Fighter Pilots. Moreover, affection may dull the edge of criticism, for they are very lovable.

'These Poles differ individually as much as one Englishman differs from another, but they have some common qualities which it is the purpose of this paper to describe.

'Personal Qualities
'The Polish Fighter Pilot is imbued with the determination to exterminate Germans. All his energies are absorbed in this purpose. "The only good German is a dead German." "Don't shoot only into their engines – some may come down alive and go back to Germany after the war."

'Although it is catalogued as one of the Seven Deadly Sins, pride is the heading under which the Poles' major virtues and some of their few faults may be set out. Their pride is without vanity. Their gallantry is "not for the sake of a ribboned coat". They shoot no line. The rare Pole who beats up the aerodrome is beaten up by his chums. Polish pride includes such attributes as courage, honour, patriotism (and its younger brother, esprit de corps), self-respect, good manners, skill, determination and, at the lower end of the scale, obstinacy.

'High courage seems inborn in most Poles. Their escapes from Poland give astonishing evidence of their bravery. One or two young pilots say they need a little more training before they fight. Nearly all say, "Why all this training, training – the best training is over France". Their frequently achieved aim is to kill a German from the closest possible range, with little regard for their own safety. Implacable in battle, they are yet gentle and considerate at other times.

'The Polish fighter pilot shares the deep patriotism for which his race is famed. This ardour finds further expression in the esprit de corps of the Polish squadrons and the Polish wings – a spirit spurred on by the rivalry between the squadrons in each wing.

'All who meet the Poles are impressed by their good manners. They are scrupulously polite to superior officers and to women, but at the same time natural and friendly and without affectation. The Polish officer has a keen sense of honour. This is immediately apparent in money matters. Mess bills are usually paid on the day they are issued and never later than the 10th of the month. Other debts are settled with similar promptitude. They never draw a cheque that is not honoured. Poles tell the truth, even if it be to their own hurt. They may offer a laughably inadequate excuse for a misdeed but never deny a wrong thing they may have done. "Clearing their yard-arm", "passing the baby" and "getting someone else to carry the can" are practises which they scorn.

'Polish pilots seldom take alcoholic drinks. This may be because drinking would impair their capacity to kill Germans. They can enjoy thoroughly merry parties without alcoholic stimulants, but on the rare occasions when drink is taken they like the party to go on until dawn.

'The killing of Germans is the ruling passion of the Poles, and there is nothing haphazard in their hatred. They fight best if they know every detail of the projected operation and have time to discuss it fully beforehand. Full discussion of an operation immediately they have landed from it they also deem essential. Taking part in a hastily improvised operation or one laid on at short notice after repeated alterations, cancellations and postponements is as demoralising to them as would be the flying of a badly designed or ill maintained aeroplane. With this thoroughness goes unhurried and unfailing punctuality.

'These qualities that have been described may be engendered by their pride. In some of the younger Polish fighters this pride is manifested in a certain obstinacy. Sometimes they are too proud to go round again and they finish up in

The top-scoring Polish unit in 1941 was No 308 Sqn, under Sqn Ldr Pisarek, but photographs of its aircraft from the period are much harder to find than those of the famous No 303 Sqn. This fighter, coded ZF-C and photographed in the summer of 1941, is probably Spitfire IIB P8317 in which Plt Off Surma was credited with an 'Me 109' destroyed during 'Circus 58' on 22 July. However, it could also be his earlier mount, Spitfire IIA P7845, which he used to share in the destruction of some 'Me 109s' parked at Guines during a 'Rhubarb' on 27 June

A visiting sailor poses in a seemingly anonymous Spitfire IIB of No 306 Sqn. The code UZ-Y was applied to just one Mk IIB, P8531, which was used by Flt Lt Stanisław Skalski to claim single 'Me 109s' destroyed on 19 and 21 August 1941 ('Circuses 81' and '84'). This aircraft had earlier flown as RF-Y with No 303 Sqn, ace Sgt Bełc destroying 'Me 109s' in it on 24 and 28 June ('Circuses 21' and '26'). The fitter on the ground is LAC Kazimierz Sawicki, but the other groundcrewman remains unidentified. Sadly, most groundcrew are anonymous in period photographs, although not a single pilot would have become an ace but for their tireless work (*Lechosław Musiałkowski collection*)

the hedge. Or they are too proud to break formation when landing and break a Spitfire instead.

'Another odd failing in some Polish fighter pilots is their liability to become "rattled" by unusual circumstances. In battle they are cool and very much "all-there" tactically. But if they lose their way, or their flaps won't come down or they run suddenly into bad weather, they may get excited and do the wrong thing. Allied to this is the moment of complete aberration that seems to come without warning at least once, and may recur, in the lives of many Polish fighter pilots. In such moments a pilot has stepped from his belly-landed Hurricane and said, "The red light was showing and the siren was buzzing so I thought 'OK' to land".

'But these things might happen to any pilot, English or Polish. The chief fault of the Polish fighters, laughingly or ruefully admitted by them all, is their incorrigible loquacity on the R/T. They maintain R/T silence as long as it is essential, but as soon as speech is permitted the torrent pours unchecked, and they have, so to speak, had that frequency.

Spitfire IIA P7855/PK-K *Krysia* (Christy) was flown by three future aces in No 315 Sqn, namely Flg Off Jan Falkowski and Sgts Stanisław Blok and Aleksander Chudek. The last-named damaged it on landing at Northolt on 10 August 1941 while returning from a cancelled 'Rhubarb'. In this photograph LAC Stanisław Bączkiewicz is standing on the wing. P7855 had originally been used by No 65 Sqn, hence the *East India Squadron* titling beneath the cockpit. Before being allocated to No 315 Sqn, it flew with No 308 Sqn as ZF-P and then ZF-B, and its pilots included aces Sqn Ldr Pisarek and Flg Off Surma (*Mark Baczkiewicz archive*)

'Collective Qualities

'The Poles are a comradely community, and there seems no malice or envy amongst them. There is healthy rivalry between squadrons, and squadrons seek to outdo one another in prowess, but in battle, and in the preparation for battle, they are all for all. They are versatile and cope equally well with fighting or such essentially "team" operations as close escort for bombers.

'Discipline varies in different squadrons, but is mainly good. The standard of self-respect and cleanliness is high. Rules are not always observed unless their observance clearly facilitates the killing of Germans, but direct orders are immediately and cheerfully obeyed.

Spitfire IIB P8648/PK-M *Marysia* (Mary) was also flown by both Flg Off Falkowski and Sgt Blok, and to good effect. The latter downed an 'Me 109' with it during 'Circus 82' on 19 August 1941, and Flg Off Falkowski followed suit during 'Circus 84' two days later

'Other Characteristics

'The social, cultural and sporting attributes of the Polish fighter pilots are little manifested owing to their absorption in the war, and the absence of their womenfolk and home surroundings. They are artistic and appreciative of music. The Poles sing admirably in chorus and are seldom stumped for the words or music of a folk-song. Skiing and swimming seem to be the chief pastimes of Poles. In England they swim and play tennis and squash. For their leave they usually stay at some country house and get what shooting, riding and walking they can.

'They spend much of their time diligently learning English and pick up our language very quickly. Their sense of humour is quick and akin to our own, and they take leg pulling and ragging in excellent spirits.

'The high qualities of the Polish fighter pilots may be accounted for by their being the pick of the Polish people, for only the best could have had the courage, determination and desire to fight on that enabled them to escape from their own country, by diverse ways and through appalling hardships, to reach England. In any event, there are no fellows more admirable and lovable than the Polish fighter pilots.'

McEvoy continued to hold Polish flyers in high esteem throughout the war, and perhaps later. He had a long and distinguished career with the RAF, retiring in 1962 as an Air Chief Marshal.

WITH BRITISH SQUADRONS

The 1st Polish Wing at Northolt was not the only outfit in which Poles were adding to their scores against the Luftwaffe. The 2nd Polish Wing, then formed at Exeter and its satellite stations, also enjoyed success, although on a lesser scale. More importantly for this book, however, it was still equipped with Hurricanes, and would continue to be so until October 1941.

During the summer of 1941 Fighter Command encountered the new Bf 109F in increasing numbers. It was clearly superior in performance to the Bf 109E that had equipped the Luftwaffe during the Battle of Britain. The Spitfire I and II (to say nothing of the Hurricane) were no match for the new 'Friedrich', unlike the new Spitfire V gradually being introduced in fighter squadrons. Even before this variant found its way to Polish squadrons, some Polish pilots had flown Mk Vs in British units. The most

While Northolt squadrons continued to fly Spitfire IIs until the end of August, Polish pilots in RAF squadrons were already flying the Mk V. Sgt Adolf Pietrasiak of No 92 Sqn was the top-scorer among them, credited with six and one shared kills within ten days in July 1941. He was then posted to No 308 Sqn at Northolt, where he reverted to flying Mk IIs

successful among them was Sgt Adolf Pietrasiak. He had scored three shared victories over France in June 1940 and, 13 months after that, in just ten days between 2 and 11 July 1941, he added six kills and one shared while flying with No 92 Sqn from Biggin Hill. Pietrasiak's fifth Spitfire kill (as well as his sixth) came on the 9th during 'Circus 41' to Mazingarbe, in the Pas-de-Calais, whilst flying W3245 – his usual Mk VB. The operation was described in the 'Composite Circus 41 Report from Biggin Hill';

'The Biggin Hill Wing, led by Sqn Ldr Rankin of No 92 Sqn, crossed the French coast, No 92 Sqn at 30,000 ft and No 609 Sqn some 5000 ft below it. The wing got on to the target and had circled it once when a formation of nine Me 109s appeared from underneath, flying towards Gravelines at 27-28,000 ft. These were attacked by two sections from No 92 Sqn, with the rear section remaining up. The rear section was bounced by a formation of about six Me 109s from the sun a short while later. After the bombing the wing came back with the bombers, and all the wing came across various Me 109s – several dogfights ensued. Point of special interest – the height at which various patrols of Me 109s appear over France has been established up to 30,000 ft. The fact that plots appeared in the operations room prior to the time of rendezvous would show that the enemy were not surprised by the operation, but were in fact getting ready for our attack.

'Enemy casualties

'1 Me 109F destroyed Flg Off Wellum No 92 Sqn

'1 Me 109F destroyed Sqn Ldr Rankin No 92 Sqn

'1 Me 109F probably Sqn Ldr Rankin No 92 Sqn

'2 Me 109F destroyed Sgt Pietrasiak (Polish) No 92 Sqn

'1 Me 109F destroyed Plt Off Archer (Canadian) No 92 Sqn

'1 Me 109F destroyed Flt Lt Bisdee No 609 Sqn'

At the end of this encounter Pietrasiak's total score of confirmed kills was five and four shared, while Rankin's was seven and four shared, Bisdee's six and two shared, Archer's three and Wellum's two and one shared. All except the last-named would subsequently add to their scores. Although he never quite 'made ace', Geoffrey Wellum's autobiography, entitled *First Light*, is probably one of the best aviation books ever written.

Later that month Sgt Pietrasiak was posted to No 308 Sqn at Northolt, where he had to revert to Spitfire IIs. His only victory with a Polish squadron in Britain was scored during 'Circus 82' on 19 August 1941 in Spitfire IIB P8318/ZF-V. The action did not entirely go the way Pietrasiak would have liked though, as is described in his PCR;

'Left Northolt 19 August 1941 at 1700 hrs, escorting bombers to Lille and St Omer. After about 45 minutes of flying, when approximately near Dunkirk, saw Spitfire attacked by Me 109F. Broke away to assist British pilot. Approached Me 109F on his starboard quarter and gave him a two-second burst with cannon and machine guns. Me 109F spun down in flames. Immediately afterwards was attacked by four Me 109s. Took evasive action by quick turns. Attacked one of the four enemy aircraft and observed him perform one turn of a spin – had not time to observe damage as I was again attacked by the remaining three. A section of four Spitfires came to my assistance and the three enemy aircraft steered off. Before I could join the British aircraft I was shot down by AA fire at approximately 16,000 ft. I had difficulty in getting out of the aircraft but was successful at 10,000 ft and landed about four kilometres [2.5 miles] south of Dunkirk. After landing I swam a canal and after going about 200 yards met two French gendarmes who, discovering I was an RAF pilot, took me to a house and gave me civilian clothes.'

This report is annotated 'Madrid, 16 October 1941'. Upon return to Britain Pietrasiak wrote a detailed account of what happened to him;

'I was the pilot of a Spitfire that left Northolt at about 1700 hrs on 19 August 1941 to escort bombers on a sweep over northern France. At about 1745 hrs, while flying at 17,000 ft, my aeroplane was hit by AA fire. The tail end of the fuselage was shot away and I went into a spin and was thrown out. At the time I was about four kilometres south of Dunkirk. I landed by parachute, and the aeroplane crashed in two pieces about a kilometre [0.5 miles] south of Dunkirk, and I believe it was completely destroyed. While I was coming down the enemy fired on me with machine guns at about 2500 ft. I was not hit, but hastened my descent and hurt my arm and leg on reaching the ground.

'A search party came out after me in a motor car, but I managed to elude them by fording a small canal and hiding in a copse. A French peasant came up to me after the searchers had disappeared and gave me a cigarette. While I was talking to him two gendarmes arrived on bicycles and asked me if I was English. When I told them I was, they went off to the farmhouse, brought me some old civilian clothes and told me not to move about after 2130 hrs, as there was a curfew after that time. They advised me to try and make my way to Lille or St Omer. I walked about four miles in a southerly direction and then asked at a farmhouse for shelter for the night. There was a Polish girl at this farmhouse, and she acted as interpreter. The people gave me food and meat coupons, as well as 200 francs.

'The following morning at about 0500 hrs I started walking in the direction of St Omer, and at about 1100 hrs I called at another farmhouse, where I was given food and then taken across the canal in a boat by an Englishwoman who was staying there. I followed the canal on to Watten and then on to a farmhouse about six kilometres [four miles] north of St Omer, where I arrived about 2130 hrs. I was exhausted and stayed here three nights and two days.

'During this time the farmer's daughter had contacted the organisation at St Omer, and a man called for me and took me to St Omer by car. I remained in St Omer about five or six days, and during this time was

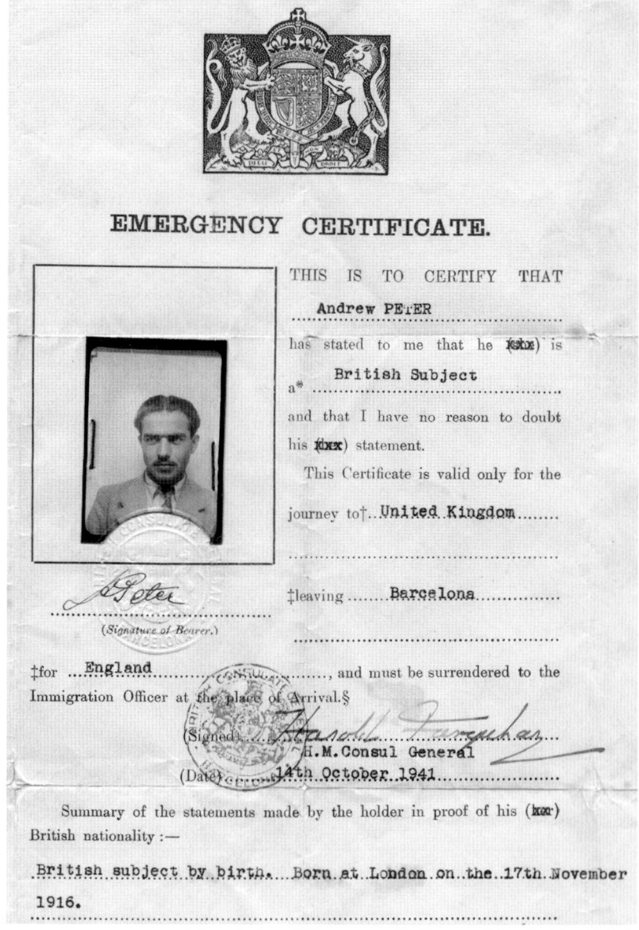
EMERGENCY CERTIFICATE.

THIS IS TO CERTIFY THAT Andrew PETER has stated to me that he (she) is a* British Subject and that I have no reason to doubt his (her) statement.

This Certificate is valid only for the journey to† United Kingdom

‡leaving Barcelona

(Signature of Bearer.)

‡for England, and must be surrendered to the Immigration Officer at the place of Arrival.§

(Signed) H.M. Consul General

(Date) 14th October 1941

Summary of the statements made by the holder in proof of his (her) British nationality:—

British subject by birth. Born at London on the 17th November 1916.

Pietrasiak's only victory with a Polish squadron was claimed during 'Circus 82' on 19 August 1941, although he too was shot down in Spitfire IIB P8318/ZF-V shortly thereafter. In a few weeks he managed to get through occupied and unoccupied France and reach the British Consulate in Barcelona. There, he was issued with this 'Emergency Certificate' that identified him as 'Andrew Peter', a 'British subject by birth. Born at London'. It duly allowed Pietrasiak to return to Britain. The ace subsequently flew with Nos 317 and 308 Sqns, but scored no more victories. Pietrasiak was posted missing over the Channel on 29 November 1943 after he had left the formation in which he was flying and turned back for England when his Spitfire developed engine trouble given new clothes. I was then taken by this man to Lille by train and handed over to another member of the organisation. I stayed with him until 2 September. Czech pilot Sgt Ptacek, Polish Cadet Stachura and an English flight lieutenant (fighter pilot), whose name I cannot remember, were also there.

'On 2 September this man and another Frenchman took us on to Bethune, where we were joined by five British soldiers. We all then went on to Abbeville by train. Here, we were given the necessary passes and corresponding identity cards to take us out of the Zone Interdite. All of us then took the train to Paris and spent the night at a hotel near the Gare du Nord.

'On the morning of 3 September we went on by train to Tours, where we changed to a local train and went about five stations farther on. We left the station in parties of two or three to walk to the river about a mile away. A farmer met us here and took us across the bridge and then accompanied us across fields for about ten kilometres [six miles] and put us on the road to Loches. From there we took a train to Chateauroux, where we arrived at about 0300 hrs on 4 September. We went on by train the same day to Marseilles, via Toulouse, arriving there about 1100 hrs on 5 September. I stayed there about a week, and then went by train to Grau Du Roi, where we were joined by several Greek soldiers. We all went out in a fishing boat to await a ship that was to pick us up. As the ship did not arrive, the Greeks went back to Marseilles and I was taken on to Nimes, where I remained for about ten days until I was called for and taken to Canet-Plage via Perpignan.

'About two days later Polish Army doctor Gasior arrived at Canet-Plage, and after a further two days Flt Lt Winskill, A L, Sgt pilot McKee, L M, and a British Soldier (a driver, name unknown) also arrived. About 5 or 6 October we left for Ax-Les-Thermes, via Perpignan. In Perpignan a Belgian pilot also joined the party.

'At Ax we were handed over to a guide who was to show us the way across the Pyrenees. We lost our way and wandered about for three days. Two days later we crossed into Spain. We walked for about 40 kilometres [25 miles] after crossing the border and spent the night at a farmhouse. The next night we went on to a small town. Here, we stayed at an inn until the following day, when a car took Gasior, Flt Lt Winskill and myself to the British Consulate in Barcelona.'

Pietrasiak was one of the first downed Polish flyers to return to Britain with the help of the French 'Organisation', but many more would follow. Statistically, a downed fighter pilot was usually either killed in the process or ended up in German captivity, but the fact that enemy-held territory was not totally hostile and there was always the hope of finding a helping hand on the ground was an enormous boost for the morale of those who continued to fly over the Continent.

CHAPTER THREE

AGAINST THE Fw 190s

The Northolt Wing received its first Spitfire Vs in the last days of August 1941, and all three squadrons had converted fully to the new variant by mid-September, flying their first operation on the type on the 16th. However, once again the Germans were a step ahead, and only five days later a completely new type of fighter was encountered, the Focke-Wulf Fw 190. On 21 September ace Flg Off Jan Falkowski claimed his fifth Spitfire kill during Circus 101 (in Mk VB W3619/PK-F), submitting the following report;

'I flew with Sgt Blok at 15,000 ft near Fruges. We were attacked from ahead by two Macchi 200s. One Macchi 200 fired a long burst at me and I noticed machine gun fire coming from the wings. I fired a short burst and almost collided with the enemy aircraft when passing by. A second enemy aircraft attacked me from my rear quarter. By very sharp turns I avoided his attack and got on the tail of the enemy aircraft. I opened fire from astern and gave him three bursts, the range being about 300 yards. The enemy aircraft caught fire and went down in a spin. I claim the enemy aircraft as destroyed.'

Interestingly, on Falkowski's original report 'Macchi 200' was underlined and 'Bloch 151' was handwritten next to it. Clearly, at the time, even the intelligence officers had not been informed about the new German type. Sqn Ldr Pisarek also scored his fifth confirmed Spitfire victory during this operation, but his opponent was the more usual 'Me 109'. Fellow

Flg Off Tadeusz Koc (pronounced Kotz, a spelling he adopted after the war) inspects one of No 317 Sqn's first Spitfires at Exeter in October 1941 during the unit's conversion from Hurricane IIA and IIBs, one of which can be seen in the background. Usually flown by Flg Off Marian Trzebiński, AD308/JH-T was also used occasionally by future ace Flt Sgt Stanisław Brzeski. On 15 February 1942, for example, Brzeski was scrambled in it when Ops Room controllers directed him and another pilot to destroy a 'bogey' approaching the English coast in bad weather. Tragically, after they had located and downed it into the sea, the aeroplane was identified as one of the RAF's first Consolidated Liberators, AM918/ G-AGDR, operated by BOAC and carrying passengers and mail on the Cairo-London route. A month later AD308 was written off during a crash-landing after 'Roadstead 12', Flg Off Stanisław Łukaszewicz escaping unhurt (*via Adam Jackowski*)

Flg Off Franciszek Surma scored five confirmed and one probably destroyed on Spitfires with No 308 Sqn during 1941, adding to his previous Hurricane victories. On 28 October 1941 Surma was decorated with the Silver Cross of Virtuti Militari and the Cross of Valour and two bars, but he was killed during 'Circus 110' just ten days later

No 308 Sqn aces followed him soon with their fifth Spitfire kills, Flg Off Franciszek Surma during 'Circus 107' on 12 October and Plt Off Jerzy Popławski during 'Circus 108A' on the 13th. When Flg Off Zumbach of No 303 Sqn reported his combat in AB976/RF-D during the latter operation, he still did not know what to call the new fighter. The relevant part of his PCR read as follows;

'Two to three miles from the French Coast, I saw three single-seater radial-engined machines (very similar to Curtiss Hawk) behind and above me. Closing to 400 yards, they dived on me and I had to break away. While diving I got under the tail of one single-seater radial-engined fighter and gave it a short burst from 100 yards range – immediately thick black smoke came streaming from it. When I pulled out of a dive, one of the single-seater radial-engined fighters fired a burst and a stray bullet severed the air-pressure pipe that operates my guns. With the guns useless, I made for home, with four enemy aircraft following. The single-seater fighters were left behind by pulling full boost and diving slightly.'

Zumbach was credited with an 'Me 109' destroyed in this operation, but his claim of a 'single-seater radial-engined fighter' probably destroyed was downgraded to damaged. It is interesting that, according to Zumbach's report, he had no difficulty outrunning the Focke-Wulf in his Spitfire V. Even more oddly, the September 1941 summary in the Combat Diary of RAF Station Northolt (prepared several weeks later, when the identity of the new aircraft was finally known) included the following passage;

'For the first time the enemy put in a new fighter – i.e. the FW 190, a radial-engined aircraft – but this aircraft was considered by our pilots to be inferior to the Me 109.'

Both assessments look rather surprising to today's researcher. It is a fact, though, that it would take several months for Fighter Command to realise how wrong it was about the Fw 190, which would soon pose a serious threat to Spitfire pilots over occupied western Europe.

In any case it was, indeed, the 'inferior' Fw 190 that was credited to Sgt Aleksander Chudek during a sweep on 21 October as his fifth confirmed Spitfire kill.

Plt Off Jerzy Popławski also became an ace on Spitfires with No 308 Sqn in 1941, claiming five 'Me 109s' destroyed and one damaged during September-November

DEADLY LOW-LEVEL MISSIONS

The autumn weather made it impossible to fly daily operations over France, but, meteorological conditions permitting, raids were flown against various targets. They included both large-scale 'Circuses' and 'Ramrods', purely fighter sweeps ('Rodeos') and also 'Rhubarb' attacks against ground targets. Still, even a 'Circus' could include an unexpected strafing attack on ground targets, as Plt Off Jerzy Popławski found out during 'Circus 108A' on 13 October 1941, when he scored his fifth kill (in AD119/ZF-X);

'I attacked a formation of seven Me 109s, and a fighter dived away towards the ground. I followed him down until, when he was about 100 yards from the ground, I gave him two bursts with cannon and machine guns from three-quarters astern on the port side, closing from 100 to 50 yards. I saw my bullets striking the fuselage. At the same moment I saw, below and ahead, a very big gun surrounded by its crew, and with what I took to be the officer in charge with his right arm uplifted. I gave a burst, saw men falling to the ground and the uplifted arm of the officer flying into the air. The gun did not fire, but I had overshot the Me 109. I had attacked and was unable to see what had happened to it. Plt Off Wandzilak, who was my No 2, saw it crash to the ground emitting dense black smoke.'

Nearly a month later, on 6 November, No 303 Sqn flew as close escort during 'Low Ramrod 5', covering eight Hurricanes attacking barges on canals between Bergues and Nieuport. On this mission Plt Off Eugeniusz Horbaczewski, in AB989/RF-C, opened his score;

'Flying as No 2 to Flg Off Bieńkowski, I shared with him the attack on the first factory, and also saw bright flames issuing from the target. Later, I gave a burst from machine guns and cannon into another factory, which was comprised of two tall containers that appeared to be connected by horizontal pipes. Later, I saw an iron bridge over a canal blow up, apparently as a result of a bomb, and some pieces of the bridge hit and damaged my wings. Near Nieuport I fired at a large water tank and registered hits on it with my cannon.

'After leaving the French coast I covered two Hurricanes, and was later warned of some enemy aircraft on my starboard side. Noticing two other Hurricanes in that direction, I flew towards them and gave them cover. One of the Hurricanes appeared to have been hit by AA or an enemy aircraft, as it was developing plenty of smoke and eventually dived into the sea. I was intending to circle the spot when I noticed an aircraft coming towards me. Its red nose showed me that it was enemy, and I turned sharply to port and met it head-on. Although it fired at me, its bullets went below me.

'I was then warned of further enemy aircraft, and saw three approaching head-on. I recognised the light blue nose of a Spitfire at the front, being pursued by two Me 109s. When I turned towards them, the two enemy aircraft broke off and turned away. The Spitfire turned out to be that of Sgt Czeżowski of No 315 Sqn. I told him over the R/T that my compass was u/s and asked him to lead the way home. Then I lost him in the clouds, and when I came out I saw about eight Me 109s at approximately 600 ft, and I again found myself over France, where much flak was coming around me. I took cloud cover, and in a gap I saw an Me 109E ahead of me, turning to starboard. Firing with cannon and machine guns with deflection, as I was approaching him I had to break off when I saw tracer bullets passing my aircraft. A short time later, however, I saw the same Me 109 again, and it was surrounded by a thick cloud of black smoke. I was then lucky enough to join up with Sgt Czeżowski again, who led the way to England and we both landed at West Malling. I only had two to three gallons of petrol left in my tanks.'

In this combat Horbaczewski was credited with the only 'probable' in his career. He would eventually emerge as the top-scoring Polish Spitfire pilot.

No 303 Sqn's Sgt Mieczysław Adamek flew a sequence of RF-W-coded Mk VBs that displayed his tally, starting with this one, AB906, which is seen here with its assigned groundcrew. It was not usual for an NCO pilot to have his 'own' aircraft like this. The five crosses in late 1941 represented two shared kills over Poland in 1939 and three more in Spitfires with No 303 Sqn

Stefan Janus had opened his score with No 308 Sqn, but his fifth Spitfire kill was credited to him after he had taken command of No 315 Sqn. His personal mount when he led that unit from November 1941 until May 1942 was Mk VB W3618/PK-J. He had a narrow escape in it on 23 November, receiving a direct flak hit in the starboard wing during the low-level 'Ramrod 12' to Bourbourg and Dunkirk. This proved to be No 315 Sqn most tragic mission of the war, as five of its pilots were killed and one badly wounded, whilst all the surviving aircraft returned to base shot up

A similar 'Low Ramrod 12' on 23 November 1941 proved the most tragic operation for any Polish squadron that year. It was No 315 Sqn's turn to fly close escort to Hurribombers on a low-level mission to a distillery at Bourbourg, and as they were leaving the French coast the whole formation found themselves over Dunkirk, exposed to ground fire from the coastal batteries and at the same time bounced by Fw 190s. Five pilots from No 315 Sqn were shot down and killed, and a sixth badly wounded – all the remaining aircraft were damaged. One of those who made it back was the newly appointed squadron commander, Sqn Ldr Stefan Janus. Having survived this disastrous mission, he scored his fifth confirmed victory during 'Low Ramrod 15' on 8 December. This time the 1st Polish Wing provided rear support, patrolling the Le Touquet/Berck-sur-Mer area. The same operation saw another ace score when Sgt Mieczysław Adamek, flying W3506/RF-U, was credited with an Fw 190. The composite combat report said;

'When about 10-15 miles from the French Coast a Spitfire was seen diving with black smoke pouring from it. Two pilots immediately detached themselves (Flg Off Gładych and Sgt Adamek) from the squadron to give protection. The pilot bailed out and they circled round the parachute while falling. The pilot hit the water but managed to climb into his dinghy and waved his hand to the two pilots, who were circling a few feet above him. They then climbed, and while circling at a height of 3000 ft Flg Off Gładych was attacked from behind by an FW 190. As he took evasive action, a dogfight developed in which Sgt Adamek took part and eventually destroyed the FW 190, which crashed into the sea in flames approximately seven miles from the French Coast. The pilot did not bail out. The pilots' full stories are given below;

'Flg Off Gładych;

'Sgt Adamek and I were patrolling with the squadron for about 20 minutes. When we left the patrol line I discovered that my R/T was not working. Ten to fifteen miles from the French Coast I saw a Spitfire diving, with black smoke pouring from it. Immediately afterwards the hood flew off and the pilot bailed out. The parachute opened, so I broke away from the squadron, followed by Sgt Adamek, and circled above the parachute. The pilot hit the water and climbed into his dinghy. While we were flying a few feet above the sea, he waved to us. Three aircraft of 315 Sqn had been with us, but flying much higher (and, as I learn now, they had lost the downed pilot).

'I wanted to check up on my R/T plug, so I climbed up to about 3000 ft, where I righted the matter. As I finished I realised that someone was firing at me, for tracers were passing me a few yards behind. I made a steep turn and saw it was an FW 190, which was still firing. On the FW 190's tail was Sgt Adamek, firing at him. I followed Adamek and climbed to protect him while he was firing. The enemy aircraft suddenly pulled upwards, followed by Sgt Adamek. This FW 190 then broke away, and I tried to get onto his tail. The enemy aircraft then dived at Sgt Adamek, but I was too far away to fire successfully. Sgt Adamek turned round, and they fired at one another head-on. I was still following the FW 190, and saw thick black smoke pouring from it. As I approached him I gave a short burst (machine guns) from 100 yards in order to finish him off, and saw him burst into flames and crash into the sea. I did not see the pilot bail out.

In September 1941 Polish squadrons at Northolt converted to the Spitfire VB. Presented by the Showman's Guild of Great Britain and named, appropriately, *The Fun of the Fair*, W3764 was coded RF-Q with No 303 Sqn and flown regularly by Flg Off Bolesław Gładych. On 24 October 1941 he used it to claim one of the first Fw 190s credited to Polish pilots

'On the way home with Sgt Adamek I saw the rescue boat about five miles from the dinghy and heading straight for him. I could not direct the boat due to lack of petrol. As I landed at Kenley my prop stopped. I was at Kenley for half an hour before I could get another battery and petrol. No claim is made. Rounds fired – 30 rounds from each of eight machine guns.'

'Sgt Adamek

'I was circling over the dinghy floating in the sea when, at a height of about 3000 ft, I saw a FW 190 diving down towards Flg Off Gładych, but I realised that there was something wrong with my microphone and I could not warn him. The enemy aircraft climbed after making the attack on Flg Off Gładych, and I followed, rapidly overtaking him. I gave a long burst (cannon and machine guns) from 100 yards dead astern. The FW 190 pulled upwards as he noticed my fire and made for France. I turned towards the English Coast, watching him all the time – then I noticed he was attacking me. I turned towards him and we approached head-on, firing at one another. I only had time for a short burst. The FW passed just over the top of my machine and then dived towards the sea. Thick black smoke was pouring from it, and as I broke away he rolled over and dived towards the sea.

'I joined with Flg Off Gładych and we landed at Kenley, later returning to Northolt. I claim one FW 190

Sgt Mieczysław Adamek in the early spring of 1942. Subsequently commissioned, Adamek flew with No 317 Sqn from late 1943 until he was shot down by flak and killed during a 'Ranger' operation on 18 May 1944

destroyed. Rounds fired – 175 rounds from each of four machine guns and 35 rounds from each of two cannon.'

Sadly, the downed No 315 Sqn pilot, Flt Lt Bernard Groszewski, was not rescued from the 'drink'. During this mission Gładych was flying No 303 Sqn's sole Spitfire VA, K9871/RF-P – the very same machine used by Flg Off Szczęsny to score his first victory with No 74 Sqn nearly 16 months earlier. It had, meanwhile, been fitted with a Merlin 45 engine, thus becoming a Mk V, but its armament still consisted of eight machine guns and no cannon.

COMPETING

The winter months reduced Fighter Command operations to a very low level. It is hardly surprising that this encouraged other forms of activity. An unusual 'firing competition' was held at Northolt on 1 March 1942, as described in a formal-looking certificate;

'RAF St Northolt
'2 March 1942
'We hereby certify that on the 1st day of March 1942 during a party in 303 Squadron of Fighters at Northolt, a box of "Lucky Strike" cigarettes was shot by Flt Lt Daszewski Antoni from a distance of 5 m [16.4 ft] on the head of Capt Wiszowaty Ryszard. The skull undamaged. Weapon type – Smith & Wesson pistol, cal. 9.'

The certificate was signed by the two flight commanders, Daszewski and Łokuciewski, as well as by Flg Offs Drobiński, Horbaczewski, Kolubiński, Lipiński, Majewski, Sobiecki (all pilots) and Gwizdalski (intelligence officer). The squadron adjutant, Flg Off Kłosin, signed a note to confirm the authenticity of their signatures and sealed the document with the round seal of No 303 Sqn. The whole event may have been influenced by the fact that an official RAF publication mentioned a 'Wg Cdr William Tell' as an example of a good shooter for fighter pilots. A cigarette box was used instead of an apple, probably because of a lack of apples in the Officers' Mess. It is not certain why Capt Wiszowaty, the Polish Army Liaison Officer, played the part originally performed by William Tell's son.

Flt Lt 'Tolo' Łokuciewski's combat career was abruptly terminated on 13 March 1942 when he was shot down in his personal Spitfire VB BL656/RF-D during 'Circus 114'. He would spend the rest of the war in German captivity

Within a fortnight of the 'competition' one of its participants, Flt Lt Łokuciewski, had been downed during 'Circus 114' on 13 March, becoming a PoW for the rest of the war, despite escape attempts.

But the wild firing contest described above was not the only one at Northolt. A much more official, and somewhat less risky, air-firing competition was held by Fighter Command's No 11 Group. The results were announced on 8 April 1942, and Polish squadrons of the Northolt Wing won by a large margin. No 303 Sqn scored 808 points (Flg Off Łobarzewski 385, Flt Lt Daszewski 203, Flg Off Horbaczewski 128 and Flg Off Kolubiński 92), No 316 Sqn came second (460 points) and No 315 Sqn finished third.

Of the four pilots of the victorious unit, only Horbaczewski eventually became an ace – it took more than just good shooting to achieve this distinction. Łobarzewski (whose personal score was better than the combined unit score for each squadron of the group, bar the best two) was soon found unfit for fighter pilot duties on medical grounds, while Daszewski (the popular 'B' Flight commander, expected to take command of No 303 Sqn) was lost during 'Circus 119', four days before the competition results were announced. It is possible that Flg Off Horbaczewski saw his demise while claiming his first confirmed victory (flying AA940/RF-B);

'I was flying No 1 in Yellow Section. The first attack by enemy aircraft was made on my squadron while turning left over the target area. Two FW 190s dived towards us and I turned right towards them. The enemy aircraft broke away from the attack and dived down, and I followed about 300 yards behind. As the enemy aircraft turned right I gave the left-hand FW 190 a short burst but saw no results. I broke away and turned left towards my squadron. I was now at 10,000-11,000 ft when I heard someone say by R/T "Attention, FW", and saw one FW 190 attacking one Spitfire from 50 yards astern. I turned right towards the enemy aircraft and at 25-30 yards range (without deflection) I gave him a long burst (cannon and machine guns). The Spitfire was now issuing black smoke and the FW 190 was still firing at it. The Spitfire then started to spin, with black smoke still pouring from it. A fraction of a second later I saw flames and then black smoke come from the FW 190, and it spun down with black smoke pouring from it. The enemy aircraft was last seen at about 4000 ft still spinning to earth *(text continues on page 45)*.

While the Polish wings at Northolt and Exeter flew operations over the continent, one squadron at a time was resting at a distant RAF station. In the spring of 1942 it was No 315 Sqn's turn. Brand new Mk VB BM597/PK-C, which was delivered to the unit in early May, was flown from Woodvale by ace Sgt Chudek and future ace Plt Off Blok. This Spitfire survives with the Duxford-based Historic Aircraft Collection, gracing the skies at airshows in Britain and elsewhere (*Mark Baczkiewicz archive*)

COLOUR PLATES

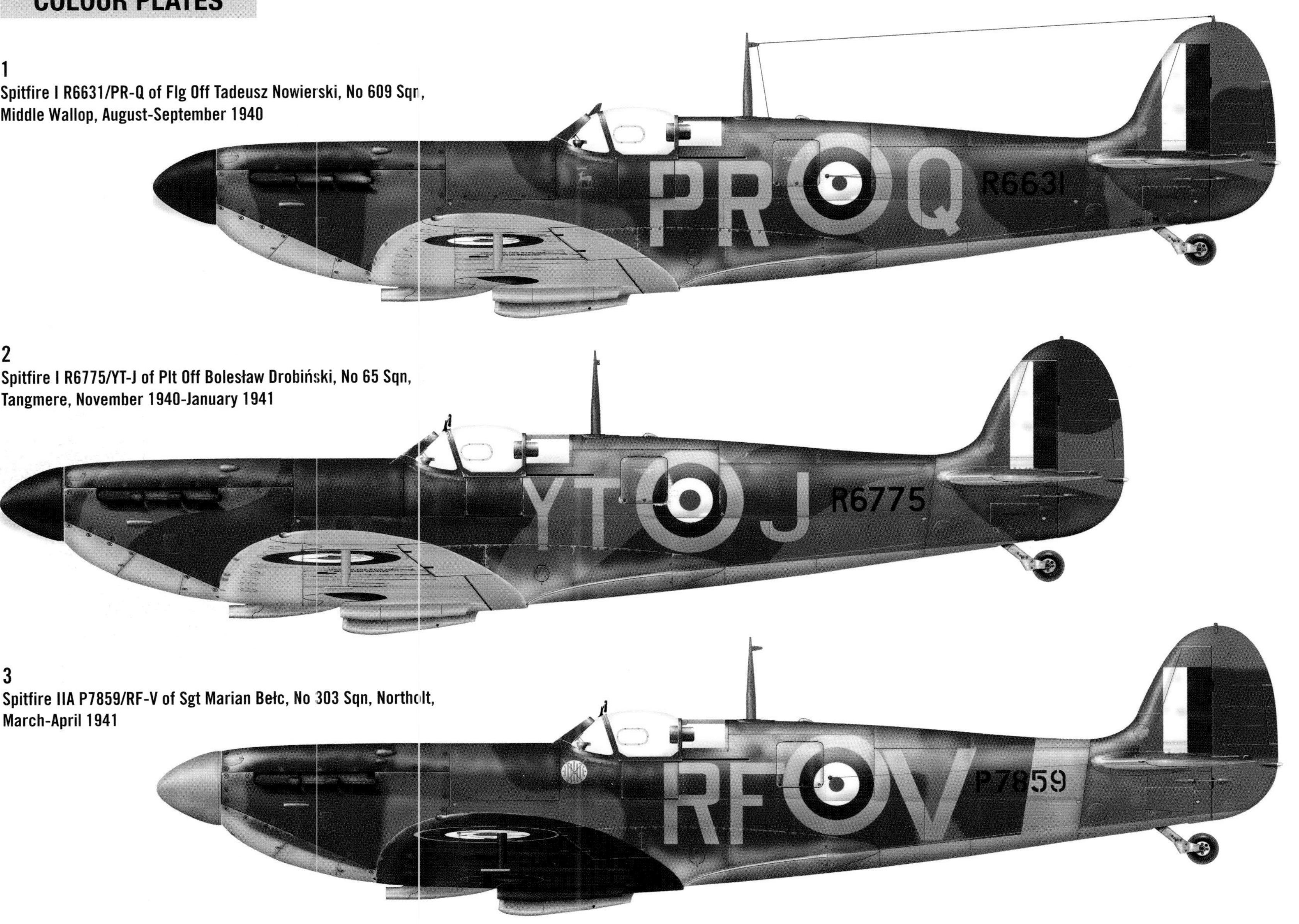

1
Spitfire I R6631/PR-Q of Flg Off Tadeusz Nowierski, No 609 Sqn, Middle Wallop, August-September 1940

2
Spitfire I R6775/YT-J of Plt Off Bolesław Drobiński, No 65 Sqn, Tangmere, November 1940-January 1941

3
Spitfire IIA P7859/RF-V of Sgt Marian Bełc, No 303 Sqn, Northolt, March-April 1941

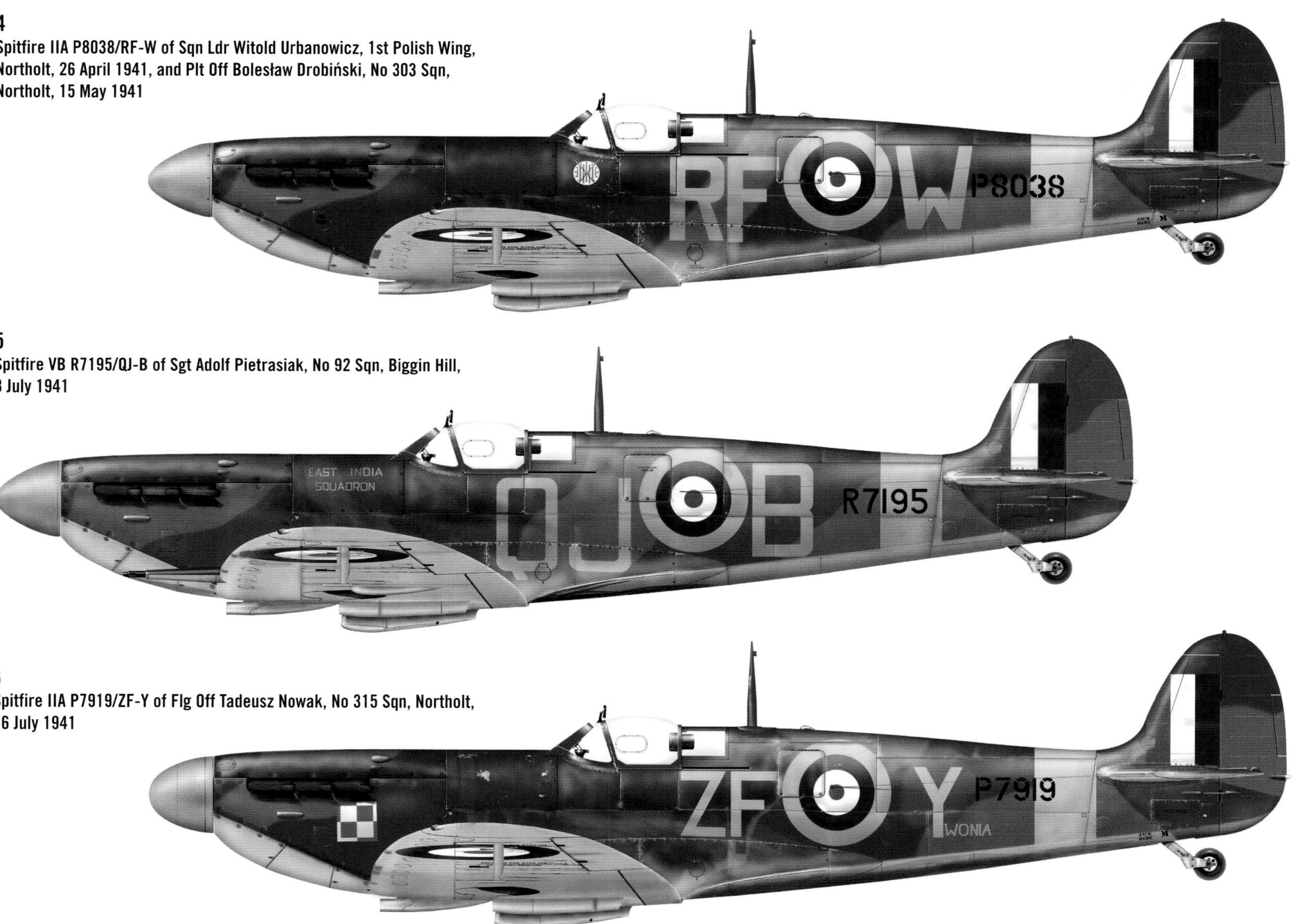

4
Spitfire IIA P8038/RF-W of Sqn Ldr Witold Urbanowicz, 1st Polish Wing, Northolt, 26 April 1941, and Plt Off Bolesław Drobiński, No 303 Sqn, Northolt, 15 May 1941

5
Spitfire VB R7195/QJ-B of Sgt Adolf Pietrasiak, No 92 Sqn, Biggin Hill, 8 July 1941

6
Spitfire IIA P7919/ZF-Y of Flg Off Tadeusz Nowak, No 315 Sqn, Northolt, 16 July 1941

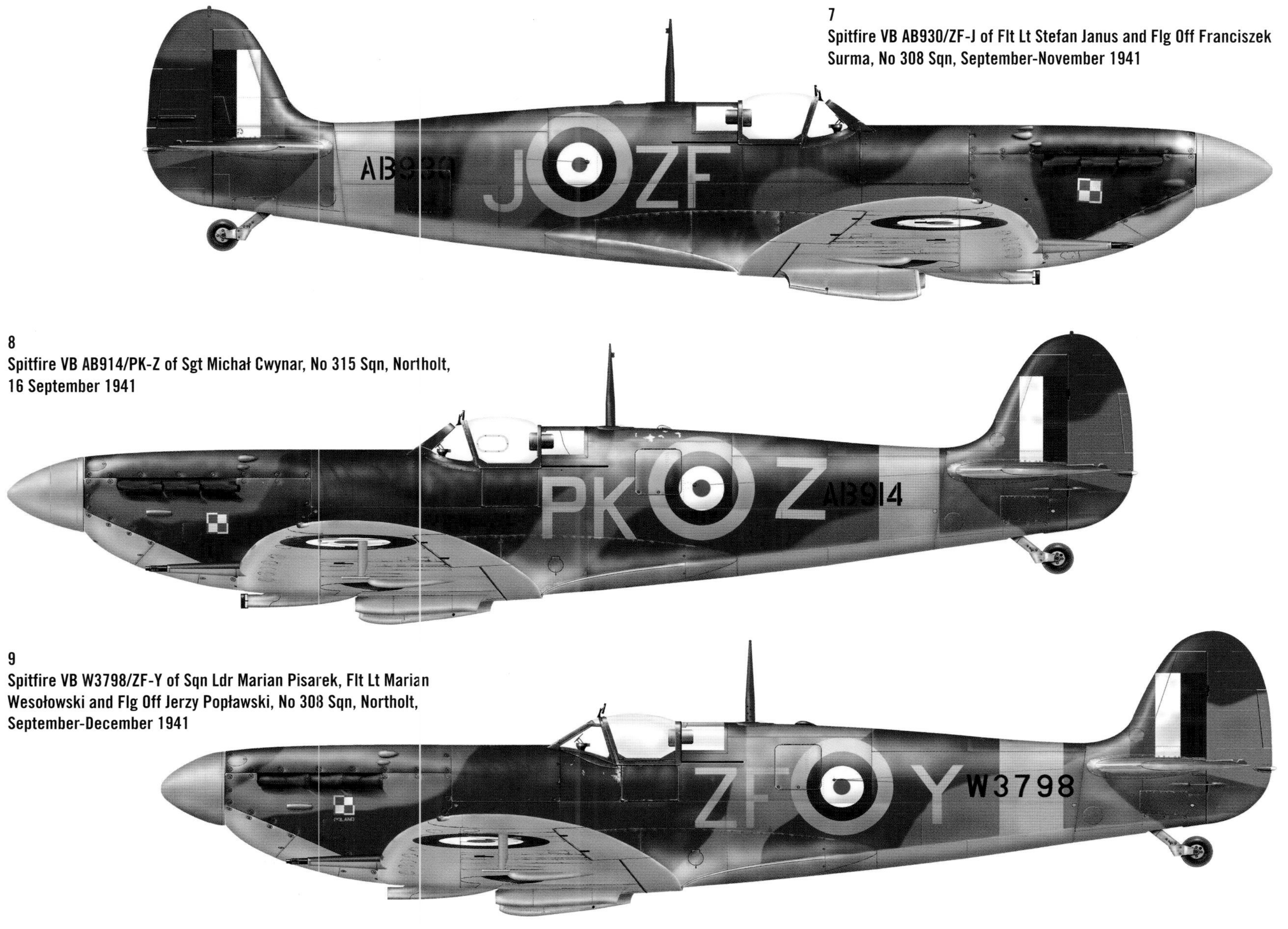

7
Spitfire VB AB930/ZF-J of Flt Lt Stefan Janus and Flg Off Franciszek Surma, No 308 Sqn, September-November 1941

8
Spitfire VB AB914/PK-Z of Sgt Michał Cwynar, No 315 Sqn, Northolt, 16 September 1941

9
Spitfire VB W3798/ZF-Y of Sqn Ldr Marian Pisarek, Flt Lt Marian Wesołowski and Flg Off Jerzy Popławski, No 308 Sqn, Northolt, September-December 1941

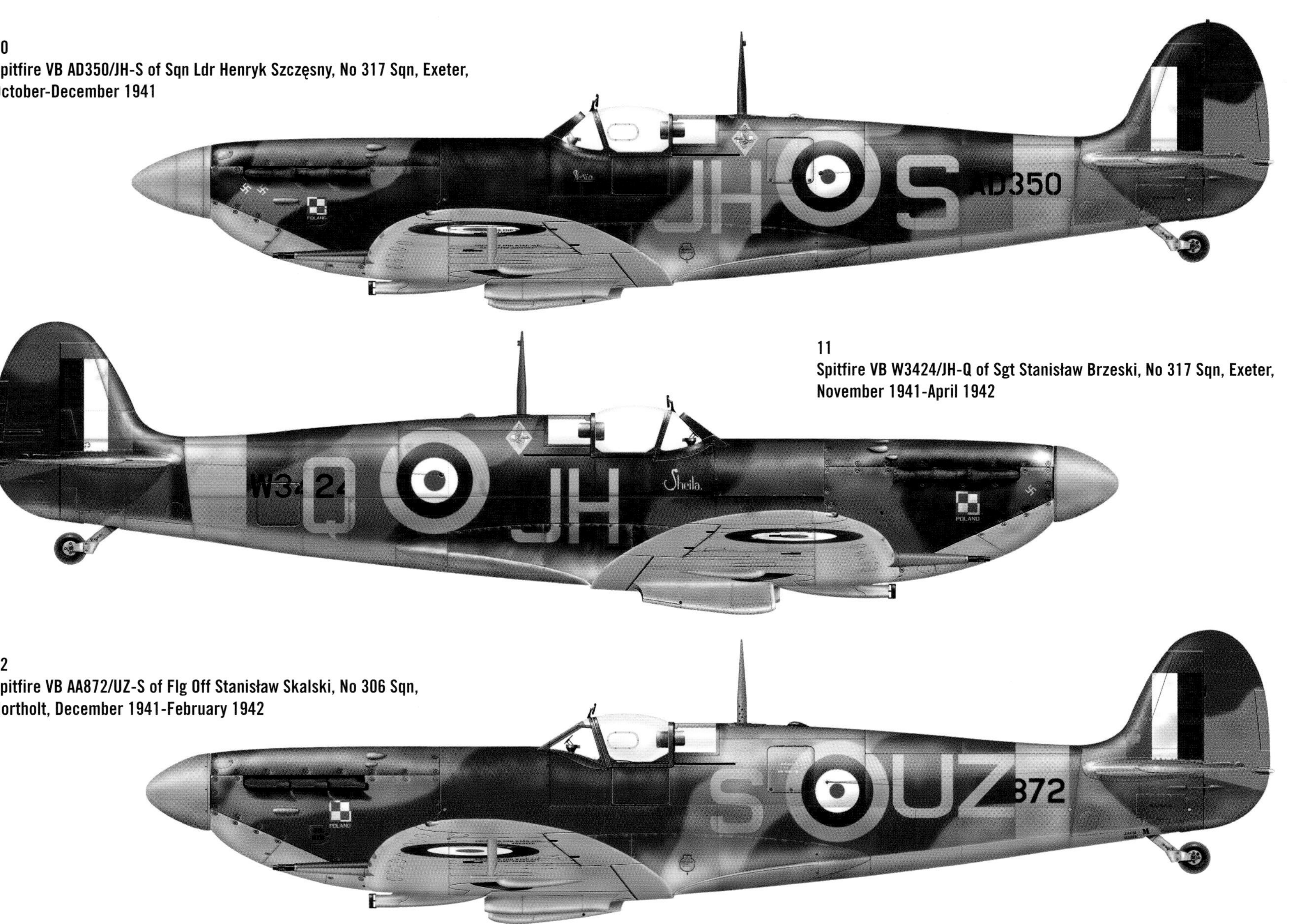

10
Spitfire VB AD350/JH-S of Sqn Ldr Henryk Szczęsny, No 317 Sqn, Exeter, October-December 1941

11
Spitfire VB W3424/JH-Q of Sgt Stanisław Brzeski, No 317 Sqn, Exeter, November 1941-April 1942

12
Spitfire VB AA872/UZ-S of Flg Off Stanisław Skalski, No 306 Sqn, Northolt, December 1941-February 1942

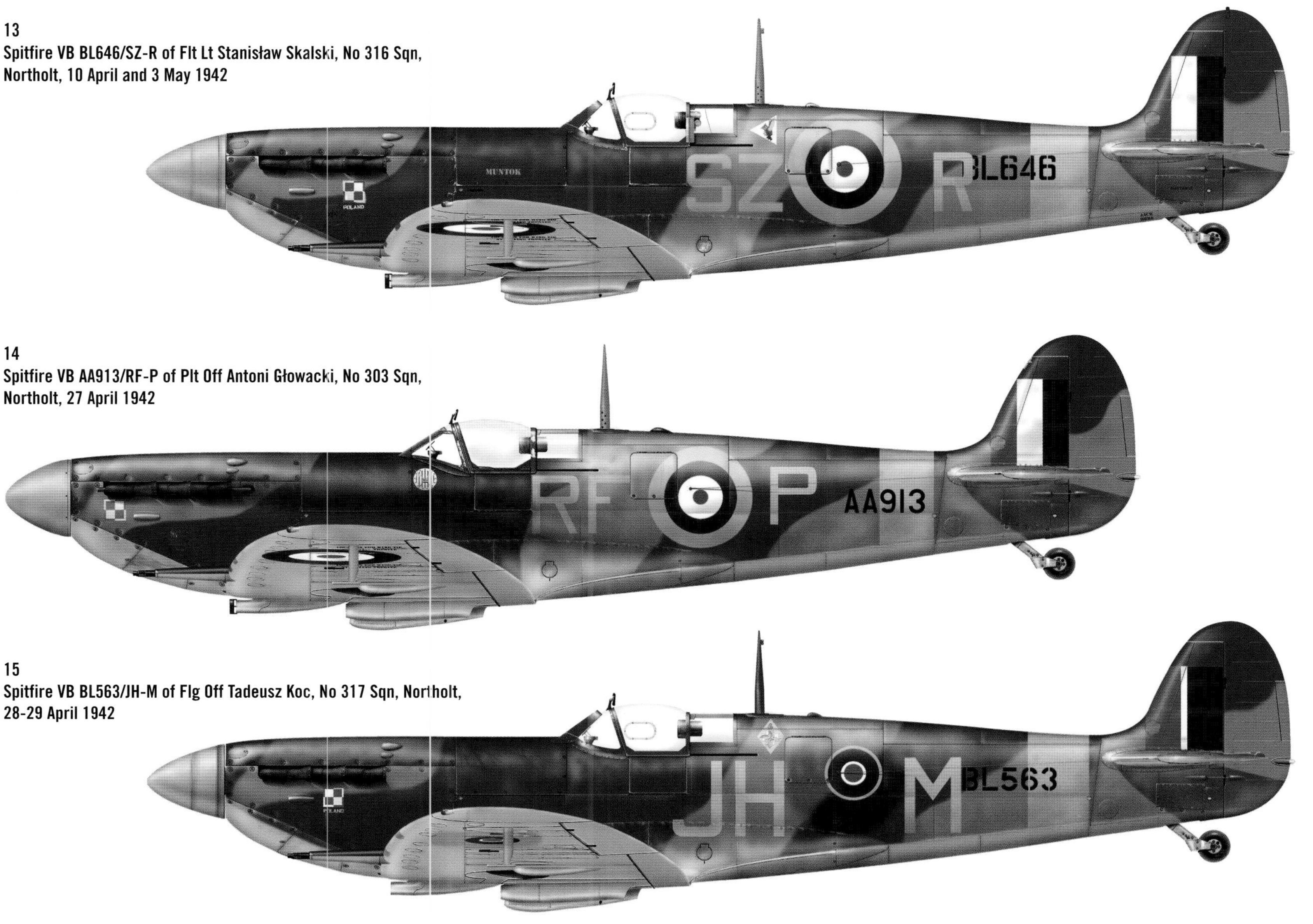

13
Spitfire VB BL646/SZ-R of Flt Lt Stanisław Skalski, No 316 Sqn, Northolt, 10 April and 3 May 1942

14
Spitfire VB AA913/RF-P of Plt Off Antoni Głowacki, No 303 Sqn, Northolt, 27 April 1942

15
Spitfire VB BL563/JH-M of Flg Off Tadeusz Koc, No 317 Sqn, Northolt, 28-29 April 1942

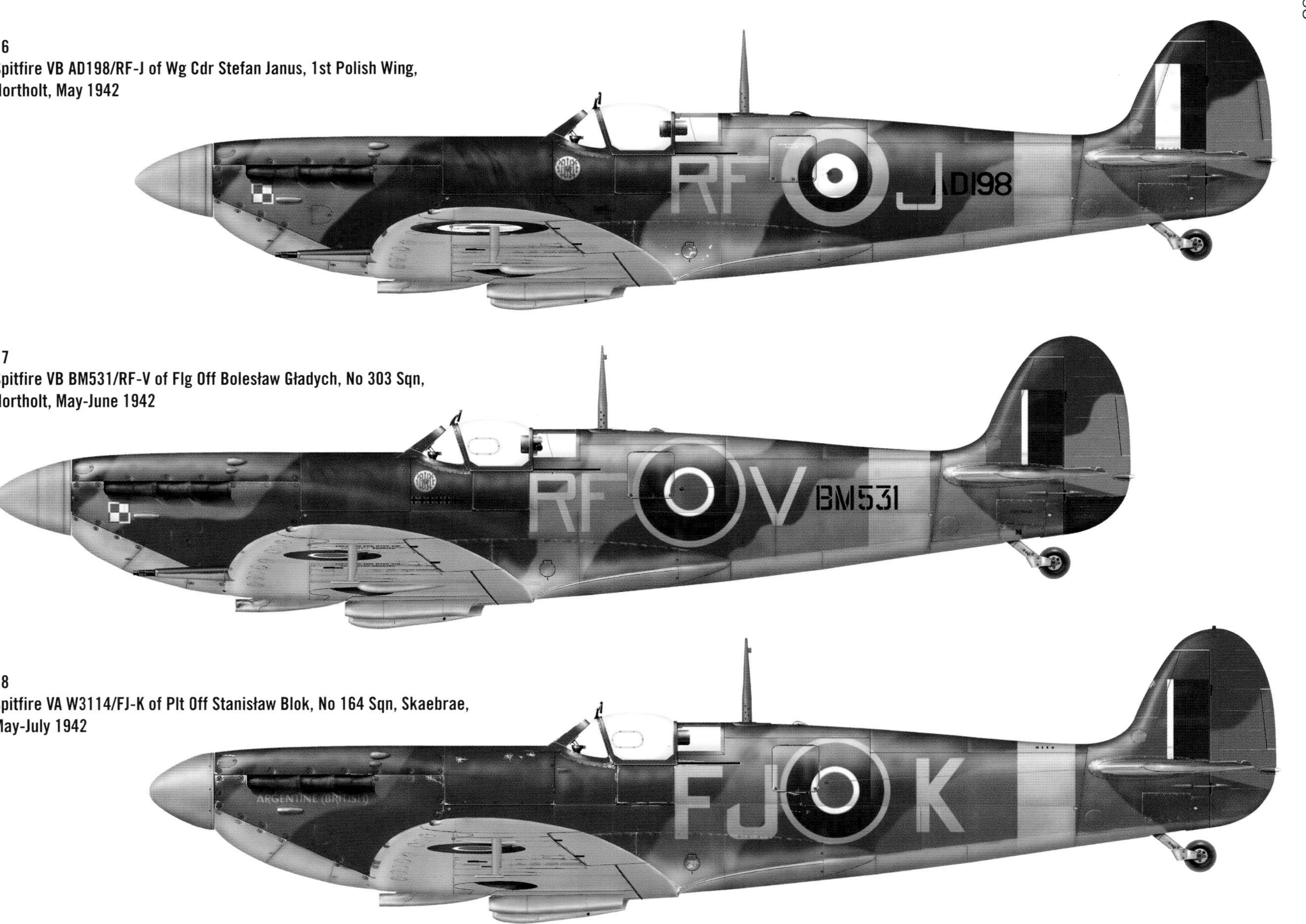

16
Spitfire VB AD198/RF-J of Wg Cdr Stefan Janus, 1st Polish Wing, Northolt, May 1942

17
Spitfire VB BM531/RF-V of Flg Off Bolesław Gładych, No 303 Sqn, Northolt, May-June 1942

18
Spitfire VA W3114/FJ-K of Plt Off Stanisław Blok, No 164 Sqn, Skaebrae, May-July 1942

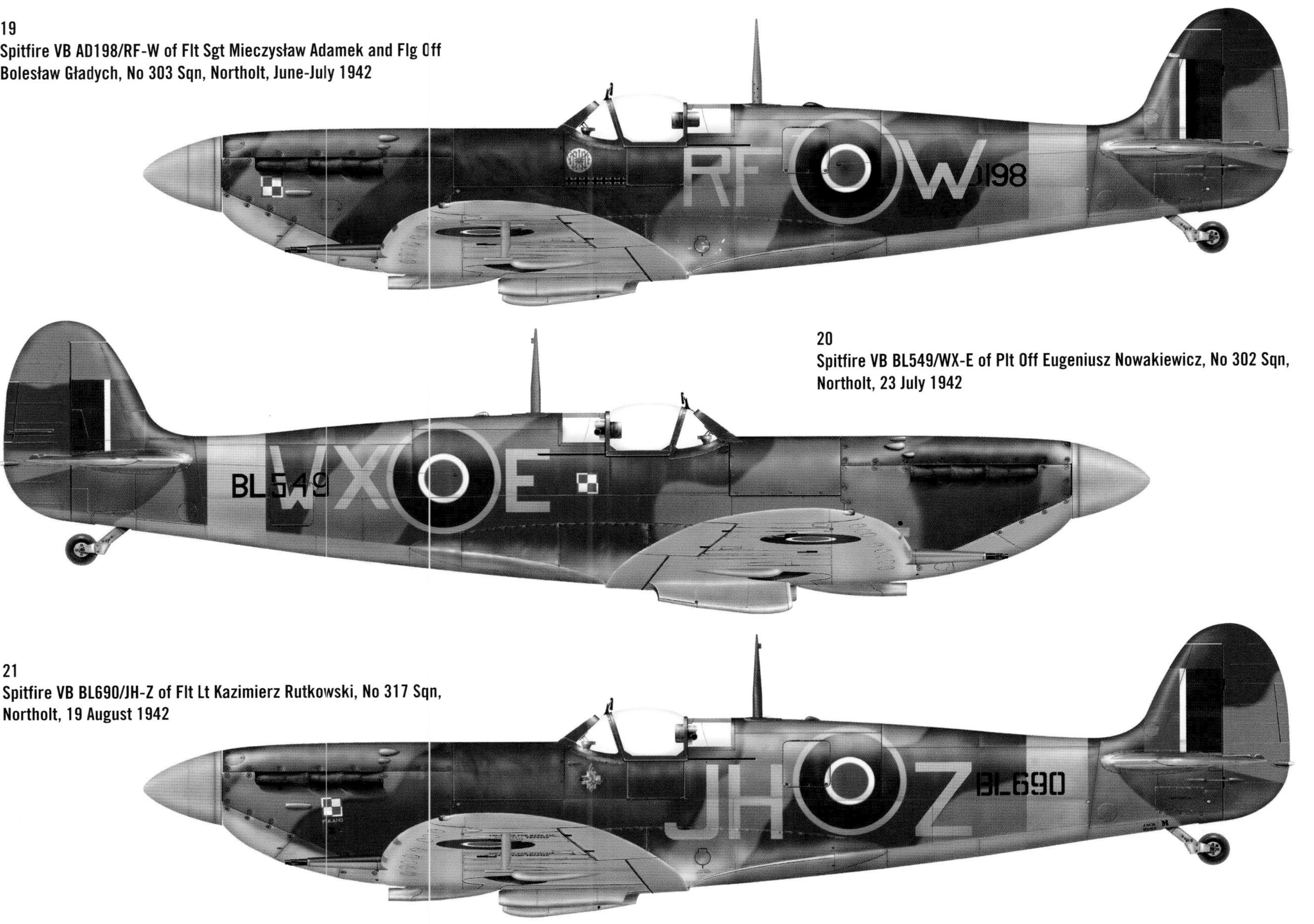

19
Spitfire VB AD198/RF-W of Flt Sgt Mieczysław Adamek and Flg Off Bolesław Gładych, No 303 Sqn, Northolt, June-July 1942

20
Spitfire VB BL549/WX-E of Plt Off Eugeniusz Nowakiewicz, No 302 Sqn, Northolt, 23 July 1942

21
Spitfire VB BL690/JH-Z of Flt Lt Kazimierz Rutkowski, No 317 Sqn, Northolt, 19 August 1942

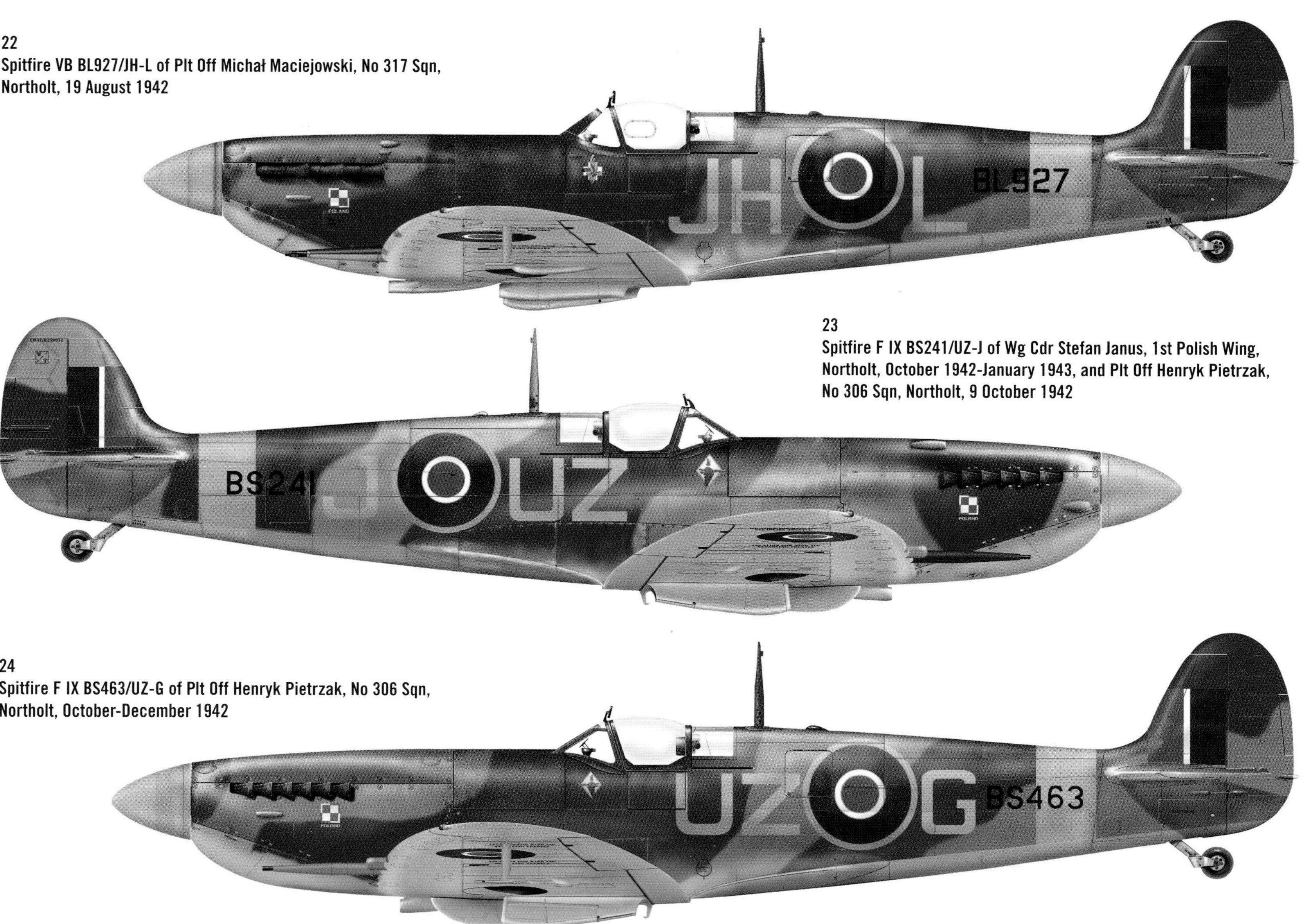

22
Spitfire VB BL927/JH-L of Plt Off Michał Maciejowski, No 317 Sqn, Northolt, 19 August 1942

23
Spitfire F IX BS241/UZ-J of Wg Cdr Stefan Janus, 1st Polish Wing, Northolt, October 1942-January 1943, and Plt Off Henryk Pietrzak, No 306 Sqn, Northolt, 9 October 1942

24
Spitfire F IX BS463/UZ-G of Plt Off Henryk Pietrzak, No 306 Sqn, Northolt, October-December 1942

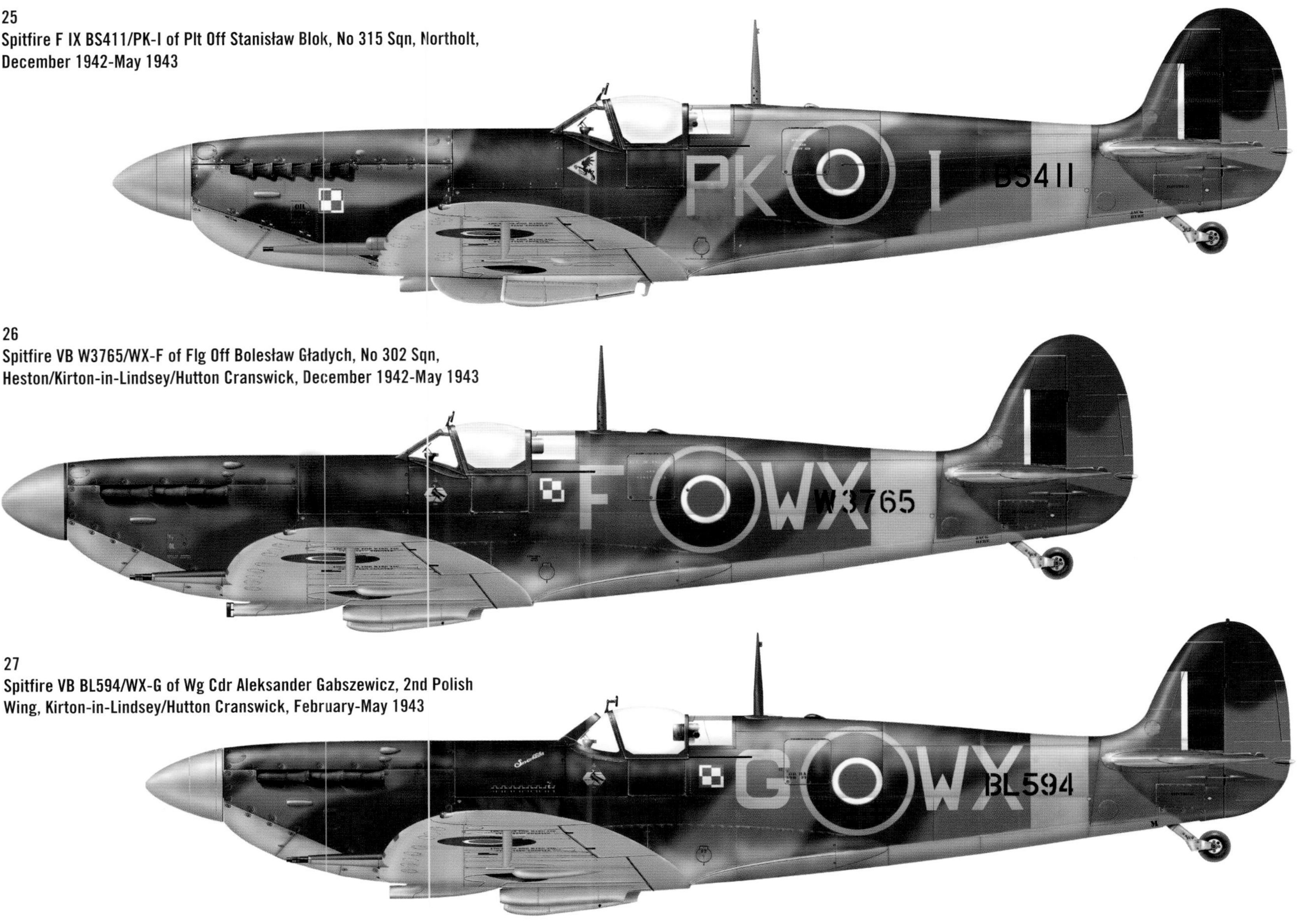

25
Spitfire F IX BS411/PK-I of Plt Off Stanisław Blok, No 315 Sqn, Northolt, December 1942-May 1943

26
Spitfire VB W3765/WX-F of Flg Off Bolesław Gładych, No 302 Sqn, Heston/Kirton-in-Lindsey/Hutton Cranswick, December 1942-May 1943

27
Spitfire VB BL594/WX-G of Wg Cdr Aleksander Gabszewicz, 2nd Polish Wing, Kirton-in-Lindsey/Hutton Cranswick, February-May 1943

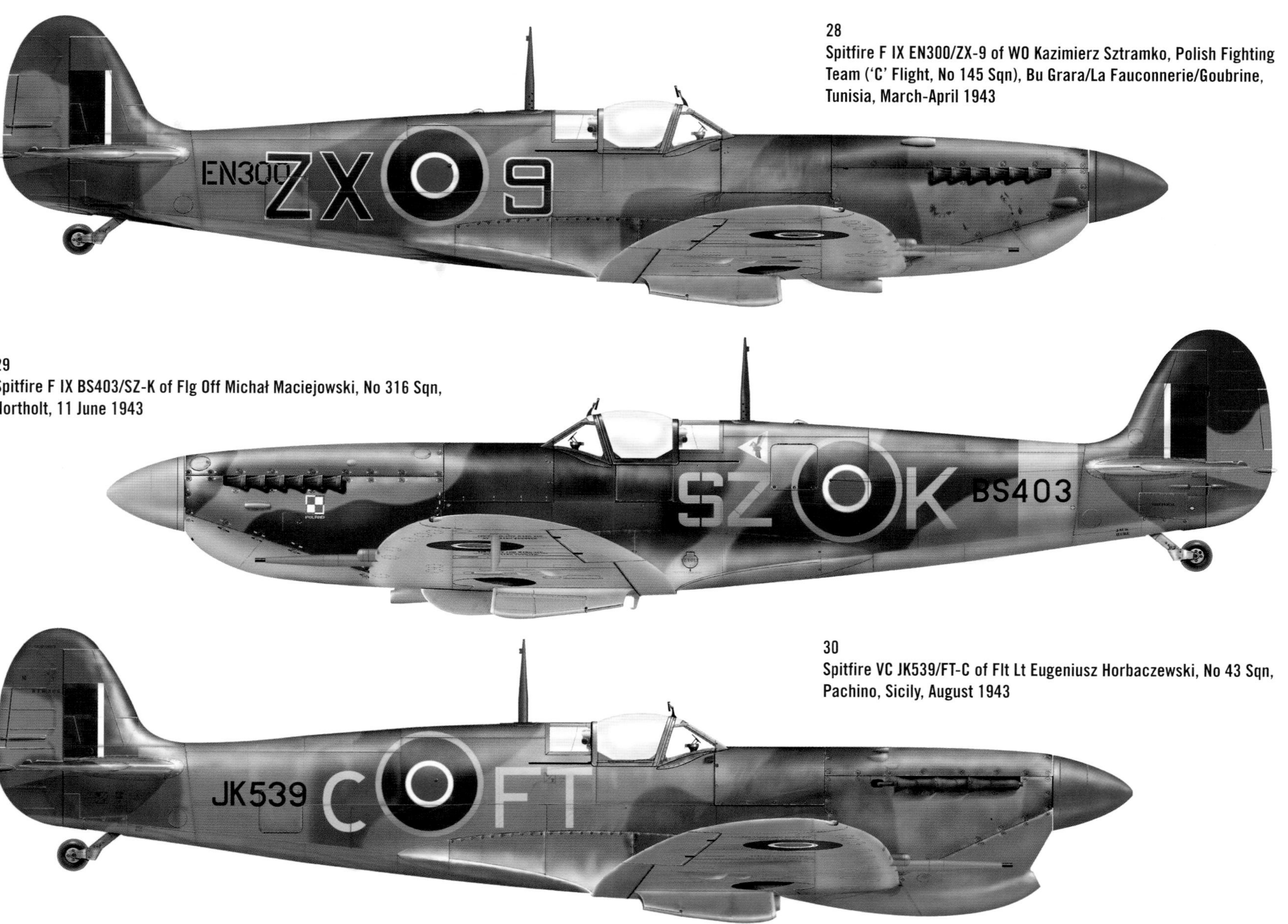

28
Spitfire F IX EN300/ZX-9 of WO Kazimierz Sztramko, Polish Fighting Team ('C' Flight, No 145 Sqn), Bu Grara/La Fauconnerie/Goubrine, Tunisia, March-April 1943

29
Spitfire F IX BS403/SZ-K of Flg Off Michał Maciejowski, No 316 Sqn, Northolt, 11 June 1943

30
Spitfire VC JK539/FT-C of Flt Lt Eugeniusz Horbaczewski, No 43 Sqn, Pachino, Sicily, August 1943

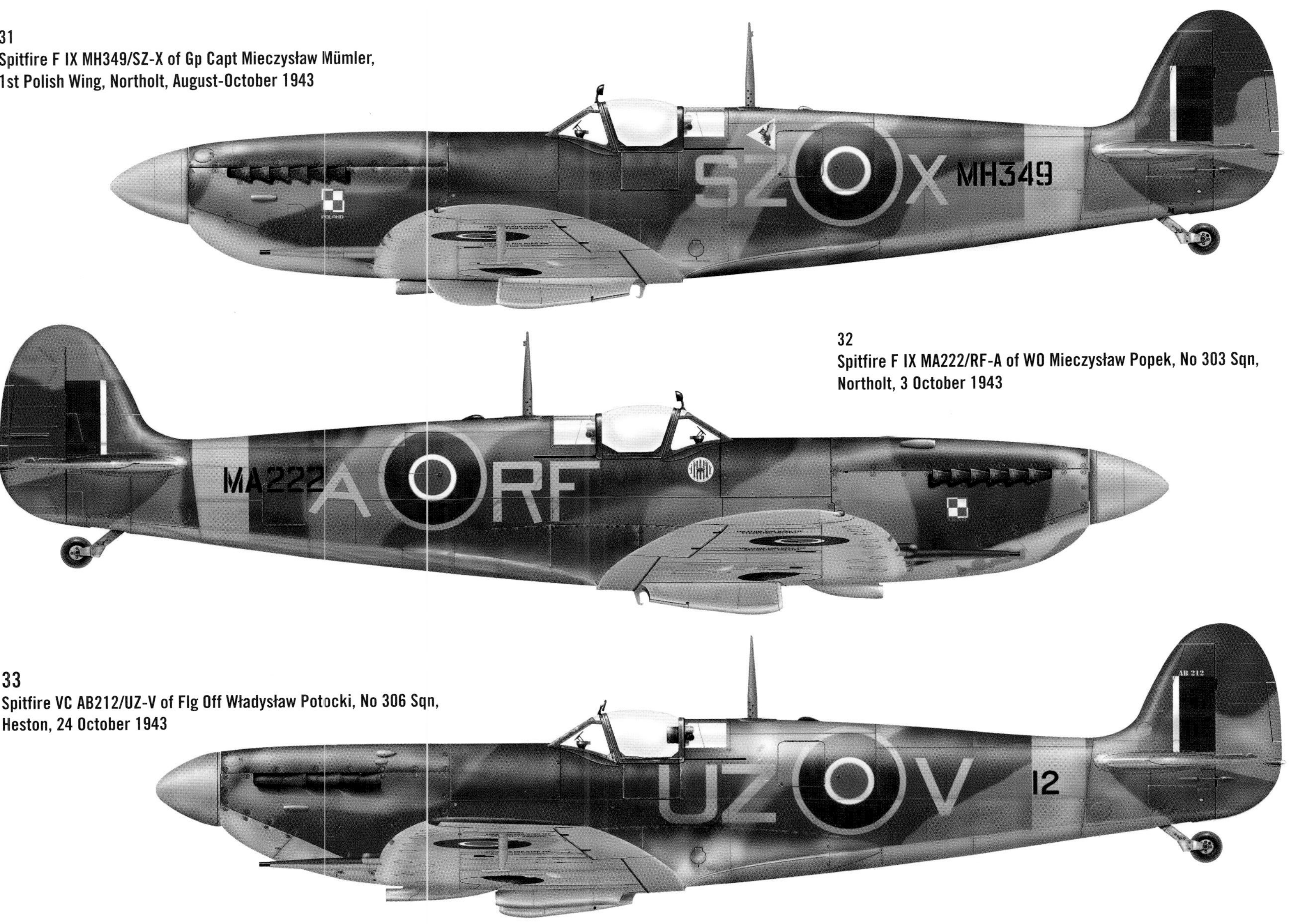

31
Spitfire F IX MH349/SZ-X of Gp Capt Mieczysław Mümler, 1st Polish Wing, Northolt, August-October 1943

32
Spitfire F IX MA222/RF-A of WO Mieczysław Popek, No 303 Sqn, Northolt, 3 October 1943

33
Spitfire VC AB212/UZ-V of Flg Off Władysław Potocki, No 306 Sqn, Heston, 24 October 1943

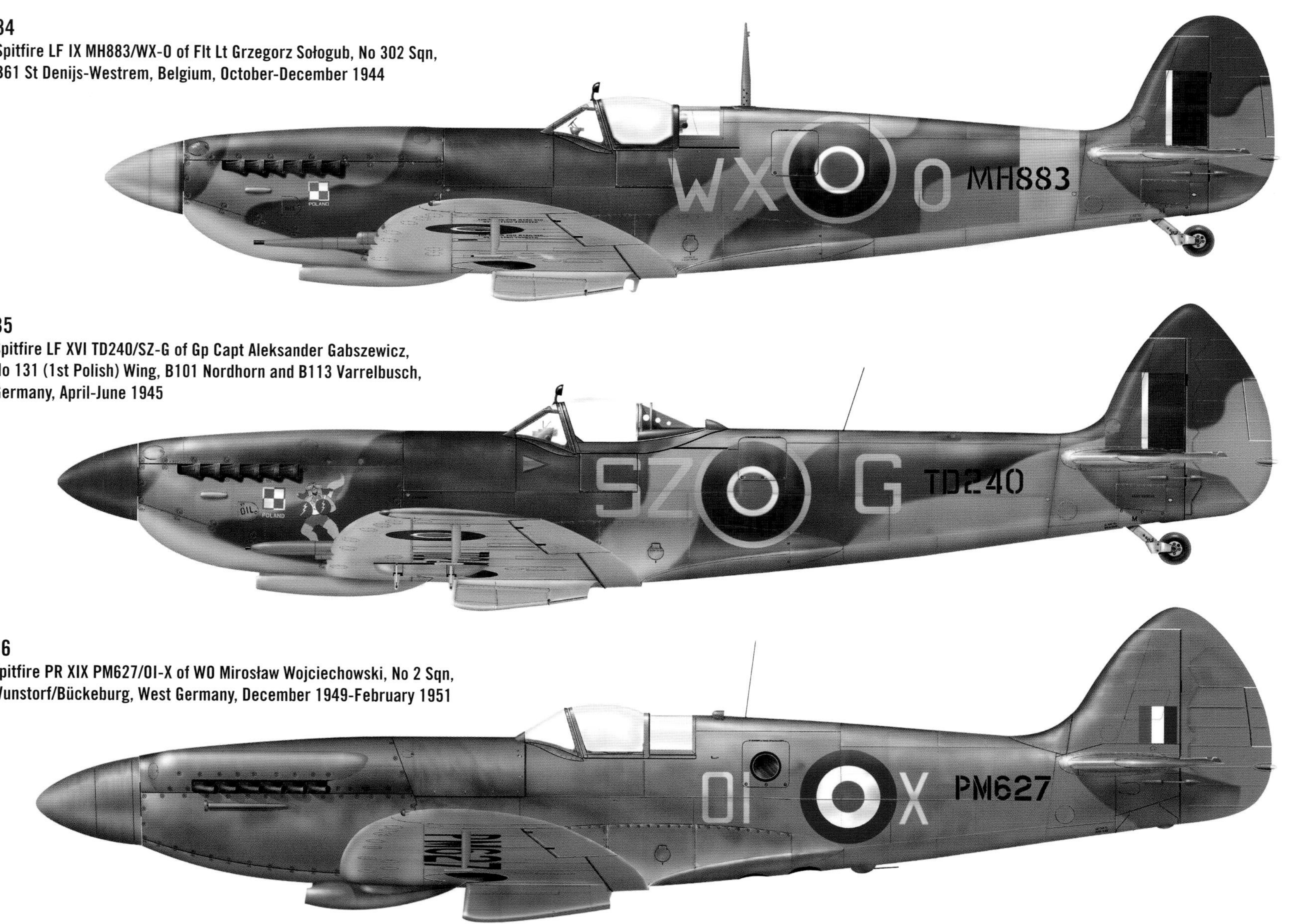

34
Spitfire LF IX MH883/WX-O of Flt Lt Grzegorz Sołogub, No 302 Sqn, B61 St Denijs-Westrem, Belgium, October-December 1944

35
Spitfire LF XVI TD240/SZ-G of Gp Capt Aleksander Gabszewicz, No 131 (1st Polish) Wing, B101 Nordhorn and B113 Varrelbusch, Germany, April-June 1945

36
Spitfire PR XIX PM627/OI-X of WO Mirosław Wojciechowski, No 2 Sqn, Wunstorf/Bückeburg, West Germany, December 1949-February 1951

'Near Calais I joined up with one [Douglas] Boston (whose starboard engine had stopped), which I escorted as far as Sandwich – I then left for base. In the middle of the Channel I was joined by Flt Sgt Popek. I claim one FW 190 destroyed.'

Oddly, as late as April 1942 Fighter Command apparently still failed to realise the general superiority of the Fw 190 over the Spitfire V (notwithstanding the fact that the latter could hold its own in favourable tactical situations, or when flown by an above-average pilot). During that month Air Vice-Marshal Leigh-Mallory, Air Officer Commanding (AOC) No 11 Group, wrote to his squadrons;

'The Germans appear to be less keen to engage our formations. I feel we are gradually getting the better of them. Stick to it and lose no opportunity to seek out and destroy them.'

So the drive to 'seek out and destroy them' continued, and two more Polish pilots attained the total of five Spitfire kills – Flt Lt Stanisław Skalski on 10 April ('Rodeo') and Sgt Mieczysław Adamek four days later ('Circus 123'). But that same month saw the entire Polish fighter fraternity dealt a particularly bitter blow when, on 29 April, Wg Cdr Marian Pisarek, only recently appointed to lead the Northolt Wing, failed to return from 'Circus 145'. It is believed that he was shot down by Focke-Wulfs.

On 3 May 'Circus 145 (rep)' operation was flown, and No 316 Sqn's 'B' Flight commander, Flt Lt Stanisław Skalski (flying BL646/SZ-R), reported;

'I was leader of the Northolt Wing which took part in a diversionary sweep in Circus 145. Biggin Hill and Kenley were the wings below us. Several times I was warned by Operations that small formations of enemy aircraft were in our vicinity. Between Audruicq and Guines four FW 190 approached from the northeast at 27,000 ft on our starboard side, making smoke trails. My squadron was at this time flying at 25,000 ft, and I warned all our pilots that the enemy was approaching to attack from the rear – I was flying in the sun about 2000 ft above and slightly behind one of the Biggin Hill squadrons. I asked Operations to warn Biggin Hill that enemy aircraft were behind them, but it was too late, as one of the FW 190s dived on them.

'Seeing that Biggin Hill did not react in any way to this attack, I ordered my pilots to turn right while I attacked the diving FW 190 that was about 150-200 yards behind a Spitfire. I opened fire from about 500 yards, as I wanted to prevent the German pilot from getting in his fire. Making a three-quarter beam attack from above and closing to about 300 yards, I got in three bursts with cannon and machine guns. The FW 190 did not fire at the Spitfire, and after my third burst the enemy aircraft went into a spin, evidently out of control. I was unable to follow it as 20-25 FW 190s were now positioning themselves to attack. I therefore ordered all our pilots to form a defensive circle flying to the right into the sun – about eight or nine FW 190s dived on 303 Sqn, flying just above us.

'I observed one enemy aircraft attack a Spitfire from this squadron and I think his oxygen bottle must have been hit – shortly afterwards the pilot bailed out southeast of Calais.

'Immediately after the first attack a second one followed, but it did not develop as the enemy aircraft at the last moment broke away and climbed back into the sun. In the meantime Operations ordered me to withdraw over the Channel owing to large numbers of enemy aircraft above us.

Crossing the French coast near Calais, I flew as far as Dunkirk with the intention of covering the withdrawal of our forces. Near Gravelines I observed several aircraft flying below and to starboard on their way to the English coast. I then set course for Dover.

'I should like to draw attention to the flying of the English squadrons. In line astern formation, they should keep a much better lookout behind them if heavy casualties are to be avoided, as I am certain that no pilot reacted to the attack described above. If I had not intervened at least two pilots would have failed to return.

'I claim one FW 190 as probably destroyed, firing as I did from fairly long range and the whole action only lasting a few seconds. Cine camera gun carried and exposed.'

A month later Flg Off Bolesław Gładych scored his fifth 'confirmed destroyed' on Spitfires during 'Circus 188B' on 5 June 1942.

2nd POLISH WING

As mentioned in Chapter 2, the 2nd Polish Wing was formed in southwest England during the summer of 1941, with its HQ at RAF Exeter. Initially equipped with Hurricane IIs, it converted to Spitfire VBs during October 1941. At the time it included Nos 302, 316 and 317 Sqns. With both Polish Wings equipped with Spitfires, the squadron rotation circle expanded. In mid-December 1941 tour-expired No 308 Sqn moved from Northolt to Woodvale for rest, No 306 Sqn (the previous resting one) joined the 2nd Wing and the latter's No 316 Sqn went to Northolt.

Although the 2nd Wing was not as heavily engaged in offensive operations over France, every now and then it would participate in Fighter Command's 'Circuses'. Sgt Stanisław Brzeski scored his first Spitfire kill during one of these, adding to his earlier one and two shared victories with

Spitfire P8742/WX-A *Ada* was flown repeatedly by ace Flg Off Czesław Główczyński with No 302 Sqn in December 1941 and January 1942

the Hurricane whilst serving with Nos 249 and 317 Sqns. On 8 November 1941 he flew AA756/JH-Z during 'Circus 110' to Lille, and Brzeski later described the combat in his PCR;

'On the way home, five miles east of St Omer and while flying at 17,000 ft, I saw one Me 109F attacking one of the Spitfires of the close escort at 14,000 ft, below and in front of me. I dived to attack the Me 109 and fired a first long burst from above, left and astern, opening at 250 yards, and then I fired a second burst at 150 yards, closing in to 100 yards. The Me 109 burst into flames, dived very steeply and fell, burning well and leaving a trail of thick black smoke – it was seen by two other 317 pilots to hit the ground.

'Having watched him to 6000 ft, I suddenly noticed a Focke-Wulf 190 approaching, with its square wingtips and tail, and its radial engine. To attack it I banked steeply left and fired a short burst. He turned sharply right and dived down apparently out of control, swinging from side to side, and I lost sight of him at 2000 ft. A moment later I saw a Focke-Wulf 190 coming straight at me from ahead. It opened fire and one bullet hit, but did not penetrate, my bulletproof windscreen. I dived down after him, firing one short burst. At 1000 ft I set course for home. I claim one Me 109F destroyed and one Focke-Wulf 190 damaged.'

The 2nd Wing's routine tasks included intercepting German bomber and reconnaissance aircraft attempting to harass shipping. One such interception gave Sgt Brzeski, in W3424/JH-Q, his fifth and ace-making confirmed victory on 6 December. The action was described in the squadron Operations Record Book (ORB);

'Three Spitfire VB aircraft from Green Section "B" Flight took off from Exeter at 1110 hrs on an exercise flight and landed at 1217 hrs. After 20 minutes, and when over Exmouth, Sgt Brzeski, Leader of Green Section, was asked by the Exeter Controller if his section could become operational. On hearing this was possible the Exeter Controller ordered Green Section to Bolthead. At Bolthead, the weather having greatly deteriorated (ten-tenths cloud above 2000 ft and driving rain), Green Leader ordered Green Two back to Exeter, and with Green Three continued to Rame Head at Buster as ordered by the Polish Controller.

'At 1145 hrs Green Section had reached Plymouth Sound when a twin-engined enemy aircraft was suddenly seen ahead at the same height (1500 ft), flying at about 200 mph off Rame Head, following the coast to the west. Green Leader approached it with full boost and the bandit immediately adopted evasive tactics, climbing into the clouds, but not before Green One had got in a burst at 350 yards. After five seconds the enemy aircraft appeared 150 yards ahead – a Ju 88.

'During its violent evasive action, twisting and turning, Green Leader, Sgt Brzeski, identified German markings on the uppersurface of the wings of the aircraft, and at 100 yards Green One opened fire with cannon and machine guns in one long burst of four to five seconds, directed upon the starboard engine, which suddenly burst into flames. Our pilot experienced return fire from the enemy aircraft, and one bullet pierced the starboard aileron of his aircraft. Breaking off only 30 yards behind in a right climb, Sgt Brzeski saw the Ju 88 turning sharply to port and diving, as his starboard engine had broken off. At the same moment portions of the right wing and fuselage were breaking off, and two parachutes, a mine suspended

Spitfire VB W3970/JH-Y, which had reduced-size roundels, was repeatedly flown by future ace Flg Off Tadeusz Koc between November 1941 and April 1942 – including on 'Circus 110' on 8 November, when he was credited with an 'Me 109' probably destroyed. On 15 March 1942 Koc managed to land W3970 safely following the disastrous 'Roadstead 12', in which No 317 Sqn lost ten aircraft in crash-landings owing to bad weather. Koc must have had a soft spot for small-roundel Spitfires – see profile 15.

from one of them, opened to the rear of the aircraft and came down into the sea near the coast.

'Green Leader then dived and gave one final brief burst just before the Ju 88 hit the sea, one mile west of Rame Head, 500 yards from the shore. Enemy aircraft sank at once, leaving oil and fuel and an inflated dinghy on the water. Green Three spotted the mine and fired at it, but without effect. The Controller, Exeter, left Green Section circling the spot for five minutes and then gave them the order to land. Green Two had landed at 1137 hrs.'

Another duty of the Exeter Wing squadrons was to escort RAF bombers sent periodically to Brest in attempts to hit German warships there. Two consecutive heavy bomber raids against two battleships, the *Scharnhorst* and *Gneisenau*, were mounted in December 1941, both codenamed *Veracity*. Although they failed to destroy the ships, the raids resulted in fierce aerial engagements, and several Polish aces scored during these.

Flt Lt Kazimierz Rutkowski of No 306 Sqn opened his score during *Veracity I* on the 18th, when he was credited with an 'Me 109' destroyed. He added another during *Veracity II* on 30 December. The latter operation saw two aces add to their scores – No 317 Sqn's Flt Sgt Michał Maciejowski (five confirmed kills with No 249 Sqn during 1940-41) was credited with two 'Me 109s' destroyed (to which he would add later), while Flg Off Czesław Główczyński of No 302 Sqn (four and one shared kills over Poland in 1939 and France in early 1940) scored his only Spitfire victory. Two future aces also scored on 30 December – Plt Off Grzegorz Sołogub of No 306 Sqn was credited with a probable (to add to the one destroyed he had claimed in September, flying from Northolt), while Flg Off Kazimierz Sporny of No 302 Sqn was credited with his first confirmed kill.

As with the 1st Wing at Northolt, the winter season was a period of generally reduced activity for the Exeter Wing Spitfires. However, even defensive patrols could bring bitter losses. On 26 January a routine patrol over the Channel cost No 302 Sqn two pilots shot down, including ace Flt Lt Kazimierz Kosiński, whose entire Spitfire score had been claimed while flying with No 72 Sqn during summer-autumn 1941.

The elements could sometimes prove as deadly as the Luftwaffe. This was painfully demonstrated during No 317 Sqn's disastrous 'Roadstead 12' on 15 March 1942. A sudden change of weather brought fog over all available airfields, and pilots had to crash-land their Spitfires in zero visibility as they ran out of fuel. Only two of them, aces Flg Off Koc and Sgt Brzeski, managed to land safely at Exeter despite the appalling conditions, while five Spitfires were written off and five more were seriously

Before Plt Off 'Charlie' Blok flew BM597 with No 315 Sqn he had to complete a tour with Nos 603, 54 and 164 Sqns in northernmost Britain. During March and early April he was with No 603 Sqn at RAF Peterhead, where he flew Mk VB AD502/XT-Z, among others (*Alfred Price collection via Peter Arnold*)

damaged. Miraculously, only one pilot was killed, Sqn Ldr Józef Brzeziński. Accidents to other causes were also taking their toll. Ace Sqn Ldr Marian Wesołowski, commanding No 308 Sqn, was killed on 9 January 1942 when a junior pilot collided with him during a training sortie.

In addition, one of No 303 Sqn's iconic pilots, Flg Off Mirosław Ferić, was killed on 14 February when he crashed at RAF Northolt during a routine practice flight. He had just been released from hospital following prolonged illness, and it is likely that he fainted while performing aerobatics.

In June 1942 RAF Northolt's Combat Diary at last contained the entry 'it was realised that the FW 190 was a better aircraft than the Spitfire VB, and the arrival of the Spitfire IX was awaited'. Indeed, it was no coincidence that during the spring of 1942 the Polish fighter force in Britain was reorganised owing to mounting losses. The 2nd Polish Wing moved to bases in northern England (with Wing HQ now at RAF Kirton-in-Lindsey), and its principal role became that of advanced training, with only occasional operational missions. The 1st Wing at Northolt remained the only fully operational part of the Polish fighter force, and it was expanded to include four squadrons instead of three, one of them based at RAF Heston, which became Northolt Wing's satellite. As before, squadrons rotated between the 1st and 2nd Polish Wings.

Although most of the Polish fighter pilots flew with PAF squadrons, some continued to fly with RAF and Allied units, and score with them too. Oddly, though, unlike the year before, the only ace to add to his score in a non-Polish unit in 1942 did not do so flying the latest variants of the Spitfire, but quite the opposite. On 31 May Plt Off Blok used elderly Spitfire VA R6801, a converted Mk I, during a sortie summed up in No 164 Sqn's ORB;

'The squadron had its first encounter with the enemy, Plt Off Blok and Plt Off Cleverly, while on interception patrol, engaging and damaging a Ju 88 east of the Orkneys. The pilots were airborne at 1920 hrs and sighted the bandit flying east at about 1950 hrs, about two miles away, roughly 50 miles east of Orkney. After a chase due east for 10-15 minutes, the enemy aircraft was engaged and strikes were seen, thick black smoke coming from the starboard engine and flames from the port engine. The rear gunner was silenced and the starboard wingtip fell off, but the aircraft was not seen to crash.'

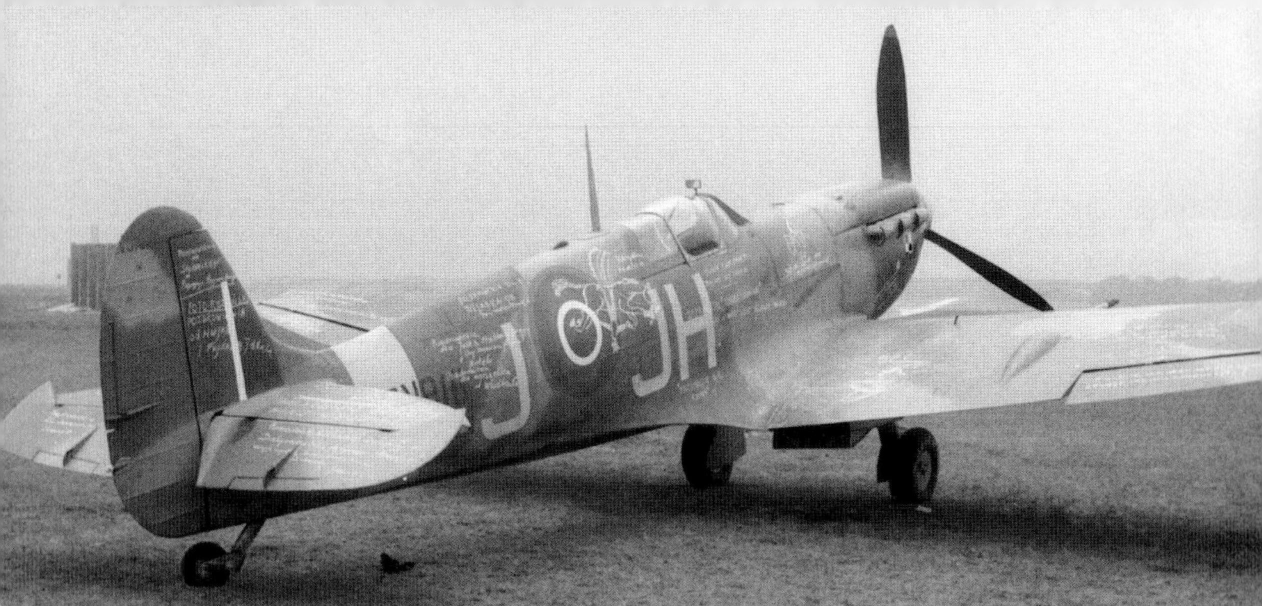

CHAPTER FOUR

DIEPPE LANDINGS

Wg Cdr Stefan Janus flew EN916/JH-J from June 1942 onwards. Like all of his personal Spitfires, it wore the standard codes of the squadron that serviced it – No 317 Sqn in this case, with the individual aircraft letter J. This photograph was taken at Woodvale in late June when Janus visited his old squadron for a party. Before he left, the aircraft was covered in chalked graffiti messages from No 315 Sqn personnel to their colleagues at Northolt. Janus was flying EN916 when he claimed an Fw 190 destroyed during 'Rodeo 81' on 26 July

In June 1942 the pattern of fighter operations changed significantly for squadrons based in the south of England. This was not only due to the awaited arrival of the Spitfire IX.

In the spring of 1942 Stalin demanded an invasion in France to relieve German pressure on the Soviets. British commanders were aware that their armies, engaged in heavy battles in North Africa and the Far East, were unable to open yet another front in France, but also that clear disregard of Stalin's problems could push him to seek a separate peace with Hitler. This led to the planning of Operation *Rutter*. Intended from the outset to end in the withdrawal of troops back across the Channel, it was seen as a probing mission to help develop optimum methods for a future invasion. Dieppe, a small port in northern France, was selected. The trial landing was scheduled for June or early July 1942, and one of the pre-conditions of success was to ensure air supremacy. To achieve that, a large fighter force was concentrated in southern England for the duration of the operation. Among others, the 1st Polish Wing from Northolt (at the time Nos 302, 306, 316 and 317 Sqns) moved to Croydon temporarily.

Air Vice-Marshal Leigh-Mallory, as the '*Rutter* Force RAF Commander', despatched a special message to his units, saying, 'We are about to take part in the first assault delivered by the combined forces of the three Services against the Continent of Europe in this war'. However, this did not happen, as explained in the July summary of the RAF Northolt Combat Diary;

White nosebands on Fighter Command Spitfires are often incorrectly linked with Operation *Jubilee*. In fact they featured on No 11 Group fighters during 4-11 July 1942 – more than a month before the actual Dieppe landings. Spitfire VB AR336/UZ-O of No 306 Sqn is seen at Croydon minus its cowling, for engine maintenance, in early July, with the bands on its nose and horizontal tailplane. During the period when these markings were applied AR336 was flown by ace Plt Off Józef Jeka, among others (*via Piotr Sikora*)

'The first seven days of the month were spent waiting for combined operations against Dieppe to take place. The weather broke up before suitable conditions were obtained and squadrons returned to their normal bases.'

During the first week of July 1942 special markings, comprising white bands across the uppersurface of the nose and tailplane, were applied on fighters assembled for Operation *Rutter*. The exact purpose of these markings remains obscure. Certainly, bands applied on uppersurfaces would serve little purpose in combined operations, where (mis)identification of friendly aircraft by the navy and the army was the primary concern. One hypothesis links these bands with Allied intelligence decoy operations, to make Hitler believe a true invasion was imminent in France. The markings, conspicuous from above, were likely to be spotted by German aerial reconnaissance aircraft. It is a fact that at about that time, at the height of the German offensive on Stalingrad, Hitler did withdraw troops from the USSR to France for defence against expected Allied landings.

Throughout July the 'combined operation' was expected, and only two 'Circuses' and one 'Ramrod' were flown by the Northolt Wing during the month. Other operations included a number of fighter-only 'Rodeos' and 'Rhubarbs'. As Northolt Wing squadrons prepared for the 'secret operation', No 303 Sqn was beginning a period of rest at RAF Kirton-in-Lindsey. Ironically, the 1st Polish Wing failed to engage the Luftwaffe between mid-June and mid-July, while the nominally resting No 303 Sqn pilots were able to re-live the Battle of Britain once more, encountering German bombers over England. On 25 June Flg Offs Bolesław Gładych and Olgierd Sobiecki were credited with a Ju 88 shared damaged, and eight days later two more aircraft of the same type were downed, as described in the composite combat report;

Wg Cdr Stefan Janus, an ace who scored all of his victories on Spitfires, led the 1st Polish Wing at Northolt from May 1942 to January 1943

'Yellow Section, 303 (Polish) Squadron (Yellow 1 Flt Sgt Wünsche [AB151/RF-F], Yellow 2 Flt Sgt Popek [BL670/RF-K]) took off Kirton-in-Lindsey at 2005 hrs and orbited base for several minutes, when they were joined by White Section (White 1 Plt Off Kołecki [AR318/RF-L], White 2 Sgt Rokitnicki [W3948/RF-C]), who were airborne at 2010 hrs. At that time there was one ROC [Royal Observer Corps] plot (Raid 301), identified by the ROC as two Ju 88s, flying at 0 ft, 40-50 miles west of Lincoln in an easterly direction. The controller, Flt Lt Ostaszewski (Polish Controller) ordered both sections over Lincoln, giving them a vector of 190 degrees, instructing them to maintain only sufficient height to preserve R/T contact. Height was duly lost to about 1000 ft, when a [Bristol] Beaufighter was observed flying at 600-800 ft.

'Almost immediately afterwards Yellow 1 sighted two bandits half a mile away, which he identified as Ju 88s, two miles east of Lincoln at 0 ft flying east. The sections were then at 500 ft. Yellow 1 warned sections of the

Two aces who spent most of their combat careers with No 303 Sqn – Flt Sgts Kazimierz Wünsche (left) and Mieczysław Popek. On 3 July they both shared in the destruction of a Ju 88 east of Lincoln, Popek flying BL670/RF-K on that occasion, when return fire damaged his Spitfire's propeller. He claimed another shared kill in the same Spitfire over Dieppe on 19 August

enemy aircraft and changed course. Yellow 1, who was ahead, attacked both enemy aircraft from quarter port astern and above, opening fire from 300-200 yards range with cannon and machine guns. His object in attacking both enemy aircraft was to slow them down, thereby enabling the others to attack with greater effect.

'Yellow 2 then attacked one of the enemy aircraft from line astern and above, from 250 yards down to 20 yards with cannon and machine guns, accurate return fire being experienced. By this time the enemy aircraft was well on fire and was seen to crash in flames at Baumber, causing some damage to farm buildings. The crew of four were all killed. Two Iron Crosses were found in the wreckage, one bearing the date of 1939.

'White Section, which had been attacking the second Ju 88, line astern and above, and 15 degrees starboard and astern from 300 yards down to 50 yards, was joined by Yellow 2. He fired his remaining ammunition at the enemy aircraft, after which he used his cine-gun, making dummy attacks until the film was exhausted. The Ju 88 was then seen to crash-land with its starboard engine on fire near Harrington. The crew (four in number) were seen to get out of their aircraft and run away, a few seconds after which there was a brilliant flash, indicating that the crew had fired their aircraft. Both sections landed at Kirton-in-Lindsey at 2045-55 hrs.

'There was close cooperation with the controller (Flt Lt Ostaszewski), who took over from Sqn Ldr Mawdesley. The highest praise is given to the ROC, accurate plots and information being received from them up to the time of the engagement.'

Two Ju 88A-4s of the 2./KüFlGr 106 (2. *Staffel* of *Küstenfliegergruppe* 106) were downed. Wk-Nr 140016/M2+BK crashed into farm buildings six miles from Wragby, killing the crew – Feldwebel H Majer, Obergefreiter H Wyborny, Unteroffizier K Schachtschneider and Unteroffizier Th Frank. Wk-Nr 140017/M2+KK belly-landed between

Plt Off Stanisław Brzeski was also credited with an Fw 190 destroyed on 26 July during 'Rodeo 81', flying Spitfire VB AR340/JH-P

Horncastle and Spilsby, and the crew was captured – Hauptmann H Bergemann, Obergefreiter B Müller, Unteroffizier E Fahning and Unteroffizier J Fickenwirth. A fin panel bearing a swastika was obtained as a trophy and put on display by No 303 Sqn. It is now preserved at the Sikorski Institute in London.

Naturally, with German bombers now seldom encountered over those regions, this engagement became quite a media event. Numerous reports with sensational headlines were published by the local press, such as 'How two Nazi raider planes which bombed houses and machine-gunned civilians and children in the North Midlands on Friday evening were brought down by Polish airmen makes one of the most dramatic air raid stories of the year'. There was an unexpected postscript a few weeks later. During their raid the Germans had strafed (among others) the Penrhos College Girls' Boarding School, evacuated to Chatsworth, in Derbyshire (fortunately there were no casualties). Parents of the girls subsequently collected £50 'in appreciation of the skill of the Polish pilots who destroyed the two planes which made the attack' and 'prevented a return visit'.

OPERATION *JUBILEE*

Eventually the landings at Dieppe, postponed by two months, were carried out on 19 August under the new codename Operation *Jubilee*. Again, as with the abandoned Operation *Rutter*, a large fighter force was assembled in the south of England. This time the 1st Polish Wing remained at its permanent bases (Nos 306, 308 and 317 Sqns at Northolt and No 302 Sqn at Heston). No 303 Sqn, at the time resting from operations as part of the 2nd Polish Wing, moved to Redhill for the operation.

Unfortunately, the intended objectives were not reached and Canadian troops suffered appalling losses. As a result of this failure, the effort of British and American ground forces was concentrated in the Mediterranean.

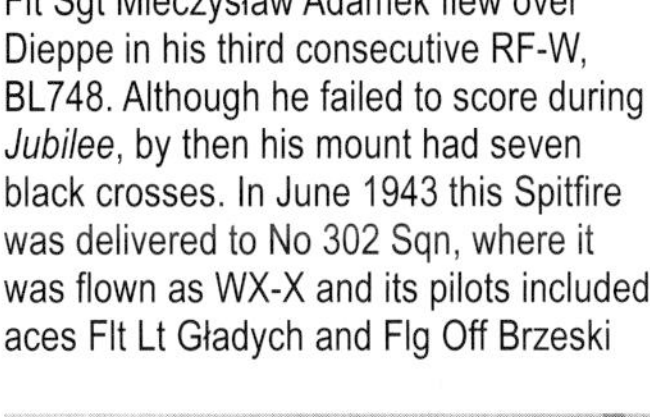
Flt Sgt Mieczysław Adamek flew over Dieppe in his third consecutive RF-W, BL748. Although he failed to score during *Jubilee*, by then his mount had seven black crosses. In June 1943 this Spitfire was delivered to No 302 Sqn, where it was flown as WX-X and its pilots included aces Flt Lt Gładych and Flg Off Brzeski

But Operation *Jubilee* was a great success for Polish squadrons, which scored 15 and one shared confirmed victories out of 96 credited that day to Allied pilots – actual German losses were about half that number. Polish losses amounted to two killed (including a Hurricane pilot in a British squadron) and one captured (of the overall total of 53 killed and 17 captured among Allied air crews).

The aerial fighting over Dieppe naturally involved a lot of fighter-versus-fighter encounters, quite similar to those fought daily during the previous year. Less usual was the concentration of dozens of aeroplanes in a relatively limited space, and the presence of Luftwaffe bombers in significant numbers, which made *Jubilee* similar to the Battle of Britain. The principal difference was that the fighting was not over England. There were also some quite new participants, as described in a report submitted by Plt Off Michał Maciejowski of No 317 Sqn regarding his late-morning mission (0930-1145 hrs) flown in Spitfire VB AD295/JH-C;

'When the squadron was over the target, making a full turn to the left, I noticed six Do 217s, two Fw 190s and a Ju 88 bombing the ships. I could not see the results of the bombing. After having released its bombs, the Ju 88 dived towards France. I dived after him from 3000 ft and gave him several short cannon bursts at a range of about 400 yards. After a short while I saw his port engine explode. The port wing and the remains of the engine broke off the aircraft.

'I made a turn to the left because I had noticed three aircraft with queer markings. At first I thought they were Fw 190s – afterwards, I recognised them as Spitfires with American markings. They joined me, and I was acting as their leader.

'When I last saw the Ju 88 it was diving out of control inland, deeper than Dieppe. With the Americans under my command, I returned to my original patrol line, where I noticed two Fw 190s attacking a convoy. I attacked the one who, after having jettisoned his bombs, was pulling out of the dive. I gave him a full burst from cannon and machine guns at a range of 200-250 yards and saw the pilot bail out.'

Maciejowski was credited with both the Ju 88 and the Fw 190 destroyed. Three other aces scored in the same combat. Sqn Ldr Jan Zumbach, leading No 303 Sqn in his personal Spitfire VB EP594/RF-D *Donald Duck*, also claimed an Fw 190, with a second one as a probable. Sqn Ldr Tadeusz Nowierski, Deputy Northolt Wing Leader flying BL860/JH-T of No 317 Sqn, was credited with two Do 217s damaged. Flt Lt Kazimierz Rutkowski, leading No 317 Sqn in his aircraft, BL690/JH-Z, claimed a Do 217 destroyed.

During the midday patrol (1245-1430 hrs) Flg Off Eugeniusz Horbaczewski, in AR366/RF-C, was credited with an Fw 190

Sqn Ldr Jan Zumbach, who was one of the more colourful characters to serve with the PAF, scored his fifth Spitfire kill during *Jubilee*. Although by August 1942 he had 11 victories to his credit, just three of these had been scored with the Spitfire. His one and one shared destroyed over Dieppe gave him Spitfire 'acedom'. Zumbach was very strict about his name being pronounced the German way – i.e. 'Tsumbach'. Apparently, pronouncing the 'Z' as in 'zoom' was an easy way of getting into trouble

Zumbach's tally was subsequently marked on his personal Spitfire VB, EN951/RF-D, in a very precise manner. Confirmed destroyed were shown as white-outlined German crosses, probables as red-outlined crosses and the sole damaged as a plain black cross. The shared category of his last kill was marked by applying 1/3 in white on the respective cross

Sqn Ldr Tadeusz Nowierski was credited with two Do 217s damaged over Dieppe as his last Spitfire claims. At the time he was the Deputy Wing Leader at Northolt, and he was flying No 317 Sqn's Mk VB BL860/JH-T on that occasion. In this photograph four groundcrewmen from that unit are seen posing with the Spitfire. Second from the right is Cpl Władysław Brzózkiewicz, remembered by squadron pilots for his competence and helpfulness (*Jim Brzozkiewicz archive*)

destroyed. Finally, Flt Sgt Popek, in BL670/RF-K, shared in the destruction of a second Focke-Wulf fighter.

The primary task of the fighter squadrons, of course, was to engage German bombers as they attempted to attack Allied ships and troops. During the afternoon mission (1530-1730 hrs) Nos 303 and 317 Sqns successfully engaged He 111s and Do 217s, as recounted in the following sequence of personal reports.

Flt Lt Kazimierz Rutkowski, leading No 317 Sqn in AD451/JH-N, recalled;

'When our squadron was over the convoy I kept it in a favourable position behind the other units. After one orbit we noticed heavy AA fire from our destroyers. Then Sgt Kolczyński [in AD269/JH-B] drew my attention to enemy bombers that were over the convoy to the left. As commander of the squadron, I gave the order for a left turn so as to get behind the bombers. The squadron dispersed and everyone was attacking on their own. I started chasing a Do 217 but, seeing some other Spitfires catching up with it quicker than I did, I turned to look for somebody else and then noticed a He 111 that had just come out of the clouds.

'When the pilot of the bomber spotted me he tried to escape into the clouds once again, but he soon gave up on this and started diving towards France instead. I dived after him, giving him a few short bursts from long range – about 400 yards. When at 200 yards I gave him another long burst, which caused the airframe to catch fire. I gave him my last burst at less than 150 yards and then all my cannon ammunition was finished.

'I was warned by Sgt Kirchner that several FW 190s were diving after me. I turned to the left, and at that moment I saw my He 111 dive into the sea. I then turned right and saw streaks in the sea where my He 111 had dived into it. Three more FW 190s started chasing me, and I had to do my best to get away by flying a series of sharp turns. I could not fire because the enemy aircraft were right behind me.'

Squadronmate Sgt Kazimierz Sztramko saw combat in AD295/JH-C;

'When I heard on the R/T that enemy aircraft were bombing the convoy I was starboard of the convoy. The squadron was ordered to turn to port. I continued my course to bring myself into a position on the right wing of the squadron, which then dispersed in pursuit of enemy aircraft. I saw a He 111 about 2000 ft above me, with Spitfires attacking it. I therefore decided not to attack this enemy aircraft. Another He 111 crossed the centre of the convoy from east to west at my altitude. I selected full boost and followed it, at which point the pilot of the He 111 saw me and tried to escape by diving. I saw two more Spitfires dive towards the He 111 from its port side, between it and me. I saw the leading Spitfire open fire, but I could not fire because these aircraft were in the way. As I turned to starboard to make a beam attack, the first Spitfire turned away to port and I fired a long burst at the He 111 from 200-250 yards.

'Then I was warned by the R/T that enemy aircraft were on my tail, and I saw tracer bullets fly past. When I turned around I saw that they had been fired by another Spitfire at the He 111 I had been chasing. Moments later I saw the He 111 hit the sea.'

For No 303 Sqn pilots the Dieppe landings were an interlude during a period of rest at RAF Kirton-in-Lindsey. From 25 July, for about a month, they were joined there by the USAAF's P-38-equipped 94th Fighter Squadron/1st Fighter Group. The American pilots lacked combat experience, and they summed up the period on departure as follows – 'Although they [No 303 Sqn] gained more experience as photographers than combat pilots in our frequent dogfights, we feel that we have learned a lot from them'. All three Spitfire VBs shown here were flown by aces while with No 303 Sqn. AR371/RF-B was the usual mount of Flt Sgt Wünsche, AA913/RF-P was flown by both Flg Off Gładych and Plt Off Głowacki and AB183/RF-A was flown occasionally by Sqn Ldr Zumbach, Flg Offs Jerzy Radomski, Eugeniusz Horbaczewski and Bolesław Drobiński and Flt Sgt Wünsche

As previously noted, Sqn Ldr Jan Zumbach was leading No 303 Sqn in his Spitfire VB EP594/RF-D *Donald Duck* on 19 August;

'When over our ships I spotted two He 111s – I ordered the port section of four to go after one, and with Flt Sgt Giermer [BM540/RF-I] I went in to attack the other. When approaching the enemy aircraft a Spitfire from 317 Sqn joined us. I fired my first burst of cannon only from a distance of about 400 yards. The He 111 slowed down and I had to break away, my place being taken by the pilot from 317 Sqn for a while. I got in another burst and finally Flt Sgt Giermer attacked the enemy aircraft until it crashed into the sea.'

Squadronmate Plt Off Antoni Głowacki (in his Mk VC, AB174/RF-Q) recalled;

'Leading the port section of four on a patrol over our ships, I noticed two He 111s approaching the convoy. The ships opened fire at the enemy aircraft and my squadron commander ordered me to attack the lower He 111. Followed by two of my pilots, I chased the enemy aircraft and fired three long bursts of cannon and machine guns, as a result of which the enemy aircraft issued black smoke from both engines and pieces began to break off. I broke away and Sgt Rokitnicki [AR366/RF-C] and Sgt Rutecki [BM531/RF-V] took up the attack, whereupon I saw the He 111 crash into the sea.'

No 317 Sqn's Plt Off Stanisław Brzeski (in BM566/JH-S) also engaged the He 111s;

'When with the squadron over the rear end of convoy I noticed AA fire from our destroyers and three enemy bombers coming out of the clouds and escaping to the south. I gave full boost and started chasing the aircraft

Photographed at Northolt during the spring of 1942, No 303 Sqn's first (and for a long time only) Spitfire VC was AB174/RF-Q. This aircraft was the usual mount of Plt Off Antoni Głowacki, who was flying it when he was credited with an He 111 shared destroyed and an Fw 190 probably destroyed during *Jubilee*

that was nearest to me. When I saw three other Spitfires attacking this machine, I went after a fourth bomber that I had noticed diving down to sea level about two miles south of the convoy. I recognised the machine to be a He 111. I attacked him from astern at a range of 200-100 yards, giving him two long bursts with my cannon until all my ammunition was finished. During my firing I saw him explode and break up. I then saw him crash into the sea after I had fired a long burst with my machine guns. He broke up completely one mile north of the French coast.'

Squadronmate Plt Off Michał Maciejowski (in BL927/JH-L) went after a Do 217;

'After having orbited once I noticed AA fire and saw a Do 217 escaping towards France. My No 2 [Sgt Adam Kolczyński] noticed him at the same time, but being in a more favourable position he caught up with him first and gave him a long burst. I followed my No 2, and when he pulled up I started chasing the Do 217. When at a range of 30-50 yards I gave him a full and long burst with my machine guns and cannon. The Do 217 caught fire and dived steeply into the sea. It crashed into the sea and none of the crew managed to save themselves.'

In this combat Brzeski was credited with an He 111 destroyed, Maciejowski and Kolczyński were each awarded a half-share in the Dornier and two trios shared Heinkels – Głowacki with his wingmen (Rutecki and Rokitnicki) got one, and Zumbach, Giermer and Sztramko the other. Thus Brzeski, Maciejowski and Zumbach scored their fifth Spitfire kills (shared ones for the latter two), Rutkowski got his fourth and Sztramko his first confirmed victory in a Spitfire. Głowacki's share in the Heinkel was his sole confirmed Spitfire kill, to add to the eight Hurricane victories he had scored with No 501 Sqn during the Battle of Britain.

LEFT Plt Off Stanisław Brzeski claimed an He 111 destroyed during Operation *Jubilee* for his fifth Spitfire kill, and his last with No 317 Sqn

RIGHT Plt Off Michał 'Mickey' Maciejowski was another pilot from No 317 Sqn whose fifth confirmed Spitfire victory came on 19 August 1942. He 'made ace' more spectacularly, however, scoring two and one shared kills during Jubilee

While Nos 306 and 315 Sqns converted to Spitfire IXs, the third Polish unit at Northolt in late 1942, No 308 Sqn, continued to fly Spitfire VBs. This one, BL940/ZF-V, was not only flown by squadron pilots, but also by senior officers of the wing. Indeed, Gp Capt Mieczysław Mümler, the Polish Station Commander at RAF Northolt, flew it on operations in November 1942 (*Paweł Tuliński collection*)

CHAPTER FIVE

SPITFIRE IXs

As mentioned briefly in Chapter 3, the Spitfire IX was seen, quite rightly, as the countermeasure against the Fw 190 scourge. The Northolt Wing received its first Mk IXs in late August 1942. Nominally allocated to No 317 Sqn, they were used to acquaint air- and groundcrews of all units there with the new variant. However, No 317 Sqn, led by Sqn Ldr Skalski, was due for a rest in the north and failed to convert

'A view to a kill'. Plt Off Michał Cwynar looks through the reflector gunsight of Spitfire F IX BS513/PK-Z, which he flew on a number of occasions with No 315 Sqn – the second unit to convert onto the F IX. Cwynar ended the war with five and one shared victories to his name, including three in the Spitfire

Capt Francis Gabreski, USAAF, hugs the propeller of Spitfire F IX BS410/PK-E, which he flew on his first combat sortie, 'Circus 252', on 21 January 1943. He had experienced real war at Pearl Harbor on 7 December 1941, but his first true combat sorties were flown from Northolt. Born to a Polish family in the USA, he volunteered to fly with the Poles to gain combat experience. In early 1943 Gabreski learned fighter pilot basics with No 315 Sqn, and he later put this knowledge to good use, becoming the top-scoring US ace of the European Theatre of Operations, and also the top-scorer among all fighter pilots who had ever flown with Polish Spitfire squadrons. Ace Flg Off Blok also flew BS410 on operations, including that of 27 February, when No 315 Sqn provided air cover for the official football international between England and Wales. This Spitfire was downed on 13 May 1943, but its wreckage was recovered in December 2005 and it is now undergoing restoration to airworthiness on the Isle of Wight, registered G-TCHI

fully onto the new Spitfire before that. When it was replaced at Northolt by No 315 Sqn, the unit's few Mk IXs were transferred to No 306 Sqn, which had now become the 'senior' unit at the station. Thus, the latter squadron became the PAF's first to re-equip fully with the variant.

Introducing the Mk IX was not the only important innovation. An entry in the September 1942 summary of the RAF Northolt Combat Diary notes, 'A most encouraging feature of this month was the increase in the number of American day bombers available for circus operations'. In fact the participation of large numbers of US bombers on daylight raids heralded the end of 'Circus' operations. The pretence of bombing enemy targets just to entice Luftwaffe fighters into battle was going to give way to actual bombings, identified by the codename 'Ramrod'. Thus far, any 'Circus' that failed to meet German opposition in the air was deemed to have failed in its primary aim, but during the next 12 months or so everybody would grow accustomed to the entirely different view that a bombing raid with no enemy fighters to intercept it was a success. Except, perhaps, for the aces.

The first victories with Mk IXs were scored in October, with one of these early successes being claimed by future ace Plt Off Henryk Pietrzak when he used the wing commander's personal Spitfire IX, BS241/UZ-J, to down an Fw 190 during 'Circus 224' on the 9th. The kills scored during this engagement brought the official score of the exiled PAF to 499. This figure has been subject to some confusion among researchers, and the author has to admit that he has hitherto followed the incorrect assumption that it related only to Polish fighter squadrons in Britain. In fact it was the total score of all PAF fighter pilots, whether flying with Polish or Allied units.

Therefore, the honour of the 500th victory should have gone to Sgt Tadeusz Turek, who scored a kill in December 1942 while flying Hawker Typhoon I R7849/PR-U with No 609 Sqn. However, although the victory was duly recorded in Turek's files, it was not acknowledged officially by PAF HQ as the 500th. This was either because the paperwork for Turek's claim became stuck in bureaucratic channels during the Christmas period, or perhaps because some high-ranking brass decided that publicity for Polish squadrons was more important. Consequently, Pietrzak's 'confirmed destroyed', scored in Spitfire IX EN128/UZ-N during 'Rodeo 140' on 31 December 1942, was generally acclaimed as the PAF fighter pilots' 500th kill. By the time this was credited, the Northolt Wing had two squadrons flying Spitfire IXs, as No 315 Sqn had converted during November.

Offensive missions were not the only operational occupation of the two units. In the entry for 10 October 1942, the No 306 Sqn ORB reports, 'Twelve aircraft flew in various formations over Wembley Stadium, where the International Soccer Match between England and Scotland was in progress'. The pilots, who included aces Sqn Ldr Rutkowski in BS459/UZ-T and Plt Off Pietrzak in BS463/UZ-G, made sure that 75,000 fans were able to watch the goalless draw unmolested.

On 27 February 1943 the Northolt Wing, including aces Flt Lt Gnyś (probably in EN179), Plt Off Pietrzak (in EN128/UZ-N) and Plt Off Blok (in BS410/PK-E) flew a similar mission, which prompted an interesting comment in No 315 Sqn's ORB;

'At 1610 hrs five aircraft took off to patrol over Wembley stadium during the International match between England and Wales. One gathers that the pilots would have preferred to fly Sikorsky helicopters on this occasion! The cockpit of a Spit at umpteen thousand feet is not recommended as the ideal vantage point from which to appreciate the finer points of the game, nor could bailing out be considered as a practical solution to the problem of getting a little closer to the game.'

This time England won 5-3, watched by their Majesties the King and Queen under the safe protection of Polish Spitfires.

Polish aces were not only providing protection for mass public events. On 11 March 1943 Flt Lt Antoni Głowacki (No 308 Sqn's 'A' Flight commander at the time) and Flg Off Józef Jeka (then a No 306 Sqn pilot) were among the attractions of the 'Wings for Victory' Week. Each made a speech to crowds gathered for the occasion in London's Trafalgar Square.

In October 1942 No 306 Sqn became the first Polish unit to fully convert onto the Spitfire IX. The unit was commanded at the time by Sqn Ldr Kazimierz Rutkowski, known as 'Śledź' ('Herring') to his friends. He is shown here with a porcelain duck, this bird featuring in No 306 Sqn's badge. The Spitfire behind him, F IX BS459/UZ-T, was usually flown in October 1942 by ace Flg Off Józef Jeka. However, Rutkowski used it on 10 October when he led No 306 Sqn aloft from Northolt to provide cover for the England versus Scotland football match being held at nearby Wembley stadium

Operations-wise, 1943 did not start well for the 1st Polish Wing. As in previous years, the Luftwaffe was not the only threat. On 26 January Wg Cdr Janus led the 1st Polish Wing on 'Circus 256', which was to be his last sortie before handing over the wing leader's duties to Wg Cdr Wojciech Kołaczkowski. It was indeed his last sortie, but it did not end as planned. His wingman, WO Wawrzyniec Jasiński, in BS459/UZ-T, collided with his Spitfire over the Channel. Unlike Jasiński, Janus was lucky to survive, although he spent the rest of the war in captivity.

SPITFIRE V CLAIMS

Although the Spitfire IX gave the Northolt Wing a new edge, two of its squadrons continued to fly the Mk V. On 3 February 1943, one of these units, No 308 Sqn, participated in 'Circus 258' – a particularly tough mission led by the Polish Station Commander at Northolt, Gp Capt Mieczysław Mümler. He later wrote in his PCR;

'After the formation had turned when it was estimated to be over the target area (Courtrai), I noticed that the bombers were now only being escorted by 308 Polish Squadron. Some aircraft from the squadron and I, therefore, drew ahead to give cover to the first box of six [Lockheed] Venturas, and a little while later I saw two pairs of FW 190s come through the cloud below and climb. They flew ahead of our formation and were then lost to sight. As I thought the enemy aircraft were manoeuvring for a head-on attack on the bombers, I took up the best position to ward off such an attack by flying on the bombers' starboard beam at their height. Soon I saw two FW 190s in front, and I therefore drew ahead of the

Gp Capt Mümler had scored four and three shared confirmed kills over Poland in 1939, France in June 1940 and in the Battle of Britain. On 3 February 1943 he was credited with an Fw 190 damaged while flying a Northolt Wing Spitfire VB on 'Circus 258'. Born in 1899, he was by far and away the oldest Polish ace to score on Spitfires

bombers to meet the enemy aircraft head-on. When 300-400 yards away I gave one short cannon burst at the nearer of the enemy aircraft, but as he flashed by me I could not see any results from my fire.

'Later, one of the Venturas began to trail white smoke, but it flew on. When, however, another head-on attack was made by FW 190s that we could not avert, another Ventura caught fire and dived down, hitting the sea and burning. In view of the fact that the assessment of my combat film shows that my cannon fire scored hits on the enemy aircraft's fuselage and tail unit, I claim one FW 190 damaged.'

Flt Lt Tadeusz Koc, No 308 Sqn's 'A' Flight commander, had mixed luck during the mission, as he subsequently reported;

'When the whole formation was over the estimated target area, where cloud was nine-tenths to ten-tenths below, it made a turn to the right. After the turn I saw six/eight FW 190s to port and behind up-sun, and warned my squadron. I then noticed that the bombers were only protected by 308 Sqn, and shortly afterwards the FW 190s that I had seen attacked out of the sun – about four enemy aircraft reached the bombers. Seeing this, I followed the last enemy aircraft but one, and at about 12,000 ft I attacked him with ten short bursts from cannon and machine guns from astern from 300-150 yards. My bullets were hitting the enemy aircraft, which emitted a large cloud of black smoke, whereupon the Hun went into a vertical dive, still smoking considerably.

'While still following the enemy aircraft I suddenly heard hits on my aircraft, and saw that a hole about three feet in diameter had been torn in my port mainplane – probably caused by an explosive cannon shell from a FW 190 on my tail. I made a sharp turn and dived into cloud, flying northwest. After five-six minutes in cloud I noticed that my engine temperature was rising, and when it had reached 130 degrees the engine caught fire. Still flying northwest, but losing height, I tried to make adjustments, but the engine revolutions decreased suddenly and I decided to bail out. I left my aircraft at 4000 ft, but as I had difficulty in finding the rip cord my parachute did not open until I was 500 ft above the ground. While falling I saw my Spitfire crash and explode. I touched down about five-six miles south of Dunkirk.'

Koc's subsequent adventures were the subject of another detailed report, filed after he returned to England;

'I came down beside a hedge near a pond and threw my parachute and Mae West into the water, after having taken the piece of adhesive tape bearing my name off the parachute. I went to a house nearby and asked for help and was refused admission either to the house or to a barn behind it, the farmer telling me that the Germans were coming. About 15 minutes after I had hidden myself the Germans arrived on motorcycles and in cars, and searched the vicinity and the houses. At about 1300 hrs the young French farmer told me the Germans had gone. He brought me food and civilian clothes. The Frenchman then took me to his house.

'In the early morning the farmer, riding before me on his bicycle, conducted me to a mill near Esquelbecq. I asked for an identity card and was given a blank form, to which I affixed an old photograph that I had had taken in Paris in 1939 for an identity card, and which bore part of an official French stamp. I completed this stamp myself and filled up the identity card. I slept until about 0400 hrs (5 February), when the French farmer escorted me to the railway station. I bought a ticket to Creil, which I chose from the map as being a small place north of Paris. I changed trains at Hazebrouck, Arras and Reims. I got a ticket for Paris from the conductor of the train merely by paying the excess fare. I speak French, though my accent is not perfect.

'I arrived in Paris at about 1400 hrs on 5 February and went by underground to the Latin Quarter, where I hoped to find an old girlfriend. As I could not find her, I returned about 1600 hrs to the centre of the city and walked round the streets and travelled on the underground. I asked about 20 people for help, but, while most of them were sympathetic, they would not do anything for me. Ultimately, I went to a hotel where I had stayed three years earlier. The woman owner remembered me and found me accommodation for the night in a house in the same street. In the morning (6 February) I got in touch with a Polish girlfriend, with whom I spent the day. She bought me some personal kit and a map of the Line of Demarcation and gave me bread tickets.

'I left Paris that night at about 2100 hrs. My Polish girlfriend had bought my rail ticket with my money. The ticket was for Jonzac and I travelled third class. I stayed in the train beyond Jonzac and got a ticket from the conductor for Dax. After passing Dax I got a ticket for Bayonne, where I got off the train. There was very strict control by French gendarmes at the barriers, but I went to the one which was most crowded and showed my false identity card. The gendarme simply looked at the photograph and at me and let me through, although he had stopped a number of French people whose cards he was not satisfied with.

'I decided to walk to St Jean de Luz. About two miles from St Jean de Luz I turned southeast into the hills, in the Foret de St Pee. I asked for food at a farm, but was given only a glass of wine. I asked the farmer for information about the frontier and he advised me to go to Ascain and cross the river by the bridge there, where the German guard was very lax. Although I was very hungry, I decided to go on – I crossed the bridge at about 1930 hrs, and the German guard did not stop me.

'I sought shelter at a house near the river, but was refused, and went on, making for La Rhume – the highest peak in the district (this peak is on the frontier). There, I went up into the mountains and, after walking for

During the summer of 1943 No 315 Sqn found itself resting again, this time in Northern Ireland. Seen here during Squadron Day celebrations at RAF Ballyhalbert on 14 August, BL670/PK-B (erstwhile RF-K of No 303 Sqn) was often flown by Flg Off Blok and Flt Sgt Chudek whilst in Northern Ireland

ten hours, by which time I was more or less exhausted, I came to a road, which led me across the River Bidassoa. I climbed into the mountains on the left bank of the river and, after walking for about eight hours, I arrived in Irun, where I asked for the "English Ambassador". I was unable to get shelter and I had no food or Spanish money. I had now been two days without proper food.

'The next morning (9 February) I walked by road to San Sebastian. I arrived in San Sebastian at about 1700 hrs and went to the British Consulate, which I entered without difficulty as the usual Spanish guard was not there. I was given 100 pesetas, and a night's shelter was arranged for me with a Spaniard. On 10 February an American officer from the US Naval Mission in Madrid took me to the American Embassy in the capital. On 11 February I was sent to the British Ambassador, and that afternoon I went on to Gibraltar by train. I arrived in Gibraltar on 12 February, and remained there for eight days.'

Koc thus established a Polish fighter pilot record for a quick return to Britain after being shot down over France. It is noteworthy that he achieved it without the help of the French underground organisation, using only his own skills and old personal relationships (female only!) dating back to his stay in that country in 1940.

RAGS

While the Northolt Wing was engaged in normal operations, April 1943 also saw a series of unusual missions, codenamed 'RAG', that were flown mostly by Spitfire Vs of No 308 Sqn. The ORB entry for 20 April reports;

'Unit detailed to act as a Russian squadron for the purpose of foxing the enemy. Rendezvoused Beachy Head at 600 ft at 1110 hrs with two Spitfire IX squadrons from Kenley. Formation flew at sea level for a few minutes, and then climbed towards Dieppe, turning, flew on to Cayeux, and returned to Dungeness, where coast was crossed at 1100 hrs. No cloud, and visibility was good. No encounters.'

The commander of No 302 Sqn, Sqn Ldr Stanislaw Łapka, cycles past his personal Spitfire VB, EN865/WX-L, which he inherited from his predecessor, Sqn Ldr Kowalski, at Kirton-in-Lindsey. On 4 April 1943 Wg Cdr Aleksander Gabszewicz led the 2nd Polish Wing in this Spitfire during No 12 Group's 'Ramrod 7', and he was credited with an Fw 190 destroyed

Ace Flt Lt Antoni Głowacki, commanding 'A' Flight, took part in this and several similar operations in April, flying his personal Spitfire VB, BL674/ZF-A. Pilots were picked for these flights from other wing squadrons as well, as the requirement was for all radio communication to be in Russian. The Poles who spoke the language fluently were accompanied on these sorties by the officer who had invented the entire hoax – Flt Lt Prince Emmanuel Galitzine, a White Russian serving with the RAF. At the time he was assigned to the high-altitude Spitfire Flight based at Northolt, and it was during conversations in mixed Polish-Russian at the Mess bar that he came up with the idea.

On 21 April a wing-strength RAG was flown by three units, namely No 308 Sqn with its Spitfire Vs, along with Mk IXs from Nos 315 and 316 Sqns. Each unit had an ace among its pilots – Flt Lt Głowacki in BL674/ZF-A, Sqn Ldr Jerzy Popławski in EN172/PK-K and Flg Off Michał Maciejowski in AB508/SZ-D. As the No 315 Sqn ORB records, the operation did not proceed as planned;

'Exercise RAG. Squadron returned when five miles south of Beachy Head on account of bad weather. This exercise was one of the culminating points in persuading the Hun that Russian squadrons were operating from England.'

It is not certain whether the point was to make the Germans think that the RAF was so weak that it had to use Soviet reinforcements, or that the RAF was so strong that it could even spare resources to train Soviet pilots. It is also not certain if German signals-intelligence services noticed it at all!

SQUADRON AND WING LEADERS

Despite such occasional shows by Mk Vs, it was with the Spitfire IX that most confirmed victories were scored by Polish pilots in 1943. During 'Circus 266' on 15 February, Sqn Ldr Kazimierz Rutkowski of No 306 Sqn claimed his fifth Spitfire kill in his personal aircraft, BS403/UZ-K. A month later his unit withdrew from Northolt for a rest period, leaving its Mk IXs for No 316 Sqn, which replaced No 306 Sqn.

The first Polish Spitfire ace, Sqn Ldr Henryk Szczęsny, had been Wg Cdr Janus' deputy in the 1st Polish Wing since late 1942. After Wg Cdr Kołaczkowski took over in January, Szczęsny continued as deputy. He was, however, destined to join his previous boss in the wake of 'Ramrod 51' on 4 April 1943. His report for that mission was not filed until two years later;

'I took off from Northolt with 316 and 315 Sqns with the purpose of escorting back the Fortresses that had bombed the Renault factory in France. We rendezvoused with them in time over the Rouen area, flying at 26,000 ft. After giving the necessary orders to the squadrons to take the arranged escort positions, and as they were being carried out, I observed

Spitfire F IX BS403/UZ-K was Sqn Ldr Rutkowski's personal mount, and he used it to claim an Fw 190 probably destroyed during 'Rodeo 156' on 21 January 1943, and another confirmed destroyed during 'Circus 266' on 15 February 1943. The latter was Rutkowski's fifth, and last, Spitfire kill, although he subsequently added to his score flying Mustang IIIs. BS403 subsequently served with No 316 Sqn

Aces had their bad moments too. At Northolt on 11 June 1943, BS463/SZ-G was pranged by Flt Lt Falkowski upon his return from 'Ramrod 87'. The Spitfire was usually flown in No 316 Sqn by fellow ace Flg Off 'Mickey' Maciejowski who, on 4 May 1943, had used it to claim an Fw 190 probably destroyed and a second Focke-Wulf fighter damaged during 'Ramrod 68'. This aircraft had previously been flown by aces in No 306 Sqn

two FW 190s preparing to attack the bomber formation. At the same time I saw two of our Spitfires colliding. I made for the attacking enemy aircraft, and after selecting the nearest one I attacked him from above and astern, firing three short bursts from a distance of about 150 yards. After my second burst I saw two bursts of flame pouring out from under the engine. The enemy aircraft went down in a steep dive emitting clouds of greyish-black smoke. Following, I gave him another burst, and shortly afterwards he hit the ground in flames.

'During this time a combat had been going on in the vicinity of the bomber formation. I pulled up with the intention of joining my squadrons. While doing this I saw another FW 190 behind and slightly below. I opened up in order to gain height rapidly, and during the climb I saw about 20-30 FW 190s preparing to attack my squadrons. I warned them at once by R/T, and also told the OPs controller, who at this same time asked me for my position. I answered "Haven't time – I am busy", as the enemy aircraft that had followed me was now in position to open fire. I was now at 30,000 ft – I decided to engage him.

'I pulled up sharply to port, in his direction, followed immediately by a starboard turn, and again a port turn in order to meet him head-on, and we collided before I had the chance to fire. He cut off a portion of my port wing and the tail – I cut off his wing and the engine caught fire. He fell to the ground in flames. My aircraft went onto its back and into a spin. My right arm and my left

Gp Capt Stefan Pawlikowski climbs out of a No 303 Sqn Spitfire. He was the Senior Polish Liaison Officer to HQ Fighter Command from 1940 until his death on operations during 'Circus 297' on 15 May 1943 – Pawlikowski was the highest-ranking Polish fighter pilot to be killed in air combat. He was also the sole Polish Spitfire pilot with World War 1 fighter experience, having flown with the French *Escadrille* SPA 86. Various accounts credit him with victories in World War 1 and later during Poland's independence wars of 1918-21, but these are difficult to corroborate elbow were in terrific pain, but somehow I managed to open the hood and I bailed out from a height of 28,000-29,000 ft.

'While descending I saw my Spitfire spinning to the ground at the same time the FW 190 was spinning down in flames. I lost consciousness twice while descending, and when I recovered I saw on my port side and below a parachute landing about 200 yards from the burning FW 190. My Spitfire dropped close to a village and the tail fell about 300 yards away. I landed about 600 yards from my aircraft. The German patrol was already waiting for me. After asking if I was a German and getting the answer that I was a Pole, they took me to an SS post. At about 2200 hrs I was handed over to the Luftwaffe, who took me to an aerodrome in the Dieppe area. I was there for three days, after which time I was sent to Dulagluft and to hospital, where I stayed for four weeks. From there I was taken to Stalagluft III at Sagan.'

Flt Lt Bolesław Gładych with his Spitfire F IX, presumably MH906/WX-V. The *PENGIE* emblem is similar to those subsequently applied to the P-47 Thunderbolts that he flew with the Eighth Air Force's 56th FG. When this photograph was taken in late 1943 Gładych's score stood at seven destroyed, two probably destroyed and a shared damaged, all on Spitfires. He subsequently scored ten more kills with the Americans

Sqn Ldr Tadeusz Sawicz was reposted to the Wing HQ to replace Szczęsny, while ace Sqn Ldr Jerzy Popławski succeeded Sawicz as commander of No 315 Sqn. On 20 April Popławski scored his last aerial success, and his only one in the Mk IX – a Focke-Wulf damaged.

June 1943 saw another reorganisation when the 3rd Polish Wing was formed by detaching the two Mk V-equipped squadrons from the Northolt Wing, which now became a two-squadron all-Mk IX outfit. At the same time one Polish unit, No 315 Sqn, moved to Northern Ireland to rest and recuperate following offensive operations.

On 22 June Nos 303 and 316 Sqns (the latter including ace Flt Lt Jan Falkowski in EN127/SZ-F) took part in 'Ramrod 99' to escort B-17s returning from a raid over the Ruhr. A signal sent subsequently by the

Sqn Ldr Jan Falkowski (right) and WO Aleksander Chudek at Northolt on 30 October 1943. By that time they had each been credited with nine German aircraft confirmed destroyed, all on Spitfires except for Falkowski's first victory. The Mk IX behind them, EN172/RF-J, was used in turn by Nos 315, 303 and 308 Sqns, and flown by no fewer than 13 aces, although only one, Flg Off Blok of No 315 Sqn, scored with it. Falkowski survived the war, but Chudek was posted missing on 23 June 1944 over Normandy in an elderly LF V

On 23 September 1943, during 'Ramrod 240', Flg Off Stanisław Brzeski used Spitfire F IX MH353/WX-K to claim an Fw 190 probably destroyed. This proved to be his last success in aerial combat. Brzeski subsequently commanded a flight of No 303 Sqn, in which capacity he was downed by flak on 21 May 1944. He spent the rest of the war in captivity

AOC No 11 Group stressed the historic significance of this operation – 'the first major daylight Fortress operation against the Ruhr'.

4 July saw another Polish pilot score his fifth Spitfire victory when Wg Cdr Aleksander Gabszewicz, who had recently succeeded Wg Cdr Kołaczkowski as Northolt Wing Leader, was credited with an Fw 190 destroyed during 'Ramrod 122', escorting B-17s on the way back from Le Mans. As the American bombers increased the pressure on German defences further inland, however, the pilots of the short-legged Spitfires had increasingly fewer opportunities to engage the Luftwaffe. The description in the Northolt Combat Diary of 'Ramrod 144' on 16 July includes a significant note – 'Many wings of Spitfires seen at all heights, but no enemy aircraft'.

Another seemingly uneventful operation, 'Ramrod 194', was flown on 12 August. The wing was led by Wg Cdr Gabszewicz in his personal Spitfire, EN526/SZ-G, at the head of No 316 Sqn, while No 303 Sqn was led by another ace, Flt Lt Wacław Król in MA299/RF-E. According to the RAF Northolt Station Diary;

'23 Spitfires (11 from No 303 Sqn and 12 from No 316 Sqn) took off from Bradwell to meet a formation of Fortresses returning from west Germany at a point ten miles north of Antwerp. However, a very strong westerly wind brought them to the rendezvous point ahead of schedule, so they continued east and eventually joined the Fortresses inside Germany, about 20 miles north of Aachen. The Fortresses were escorted back to the Dutch coast, having made a sharp turn north to avoid intense heavy flak at Antwerp. No enemy aircraft were seen so, being short of fuel, the wing returned independently to land at Bradwell and Manston. The Northolt Wing thus has the honour of being the first Spitfire wing to operate over Germany – a notable achievement, even with a strong escort of Fortresses.'

CHAPTER SIX

MEDITERRANEAN ADVENTURES

Spitfire F IX EN315/ZX-6, the top-scoring aeroplane of the PFT, was used by five different pilots to add to their scores, including three aces – Sqn Ldr Skalski, Flt Lt Horbaczewski and WO Popek. The aircraft's colour scheme remains a mystery. In a well-known sequence of photographs other machines clearly display their Desert Scheme camouflage pattern, but this Spitfire does not. Note that the swastikas applied to a PFT Spitfire symbolised victories scored by various pilots in that particular machine, rather than any specific pilot's personal tally

With a Luftwaffe presence within reach of Northolt and Heston-based Spitfires becoming increasingly rare, the idea of sending Polish fighters overseas was proposed. Such a suggestion was not entirely new, as in late 1941/early 1942 Polish volunteers had joined the RAF's famous No 112 'Shark' Sqn, with whom they fought over Libya in Curtiss Kittyhawks. They were not successful, however, having been posted in from the ferry unit at Takoradi with insufficient fighter pilot conversion training.

Now, as the RAF in North Africa was gathering operational experience in combined army/air force operations far from permanent bases, it was decided to send a group of seasoned Polish fighter pilots to that theatre. They would learn new tactics and then apply them in Polish units during the forthcoming invasion in western Europe. The group, which arrived in-theatre in March 1943, was officially known as the Polish Combat Team or Polish Fighting Team (the abbreviation PFT was used in its official emblem), but it later became known as 'Skalski's Circus' after its famous leader. Allocated to Bu Grara, Tunisia, based No 145 Sqn as its third flight for logistics purposes, it took part in fighting until May, when the Axis forces in Africa were finally defeated.

Sqn Ldr Stanisław Skalski briefs the pilots of his 'Circus' in North Africa. Listening and watching are, from left to right, Flt Lts Karol Pniak and Eugeniusz Horbaczewski, WO Władysław Majchrzyk and Flg Off Ludwik Martel

The PFT's score was opened on 28 March, as described in the following composite report;

'The flight was approaching Sfax at 8000 ft when Me 109s and Heinkels were reported below and seven Ju 88s were seen below flying northwest at 0 ft and Sqn Ldr Skalski [EN459/ZX-1] and Flt Lt Horbaczewski [EN267/ZX-5] went down to attack, the remaining Spitfires staying up as top cover.

'Sqn Ldr Skalski saw two Ju 88s flying line astern and attacked the front one, leaving the second for his No 2. He fired two long bursts from 300 yards astern and above and saw pieces fly off the port wing. The enemy aircraft heeled over to the left as Sqn Ldr Skalski pulled up past it, crashing into a building in the northwest quarter of the town. An Me 109 was reported and then seen by Sqn Ldr Skalski making off to the northwest. Sqn Ldr Skalski then flew down one of the main streets of Sfax, strafing with cannon and machine guns. He set one truck on fire. Sqn Ldr Skalski claims one Ju 88 destroyed.

'Flt Lt Horbaczewski attacked the second of the two enemy aircraft at a height of 150 ft. He fired a long burst from 400 yards and continued to fire as he closed in. At 200 yards both engines caught fire and Flt Lt Horbaczewski broke off the engagement at 100 yards as Me 109s were reported. The enemy aircraft was then flying northwest with both engines blazing, and large pieces were seen to fall off the starboard wing. Flt Lt Horbaczewski rejoined his formation and there was no further incident. Flt Lt Horbaczewski claims one Ju 88 destroyed.'

WO Kazimierz Sztramko added three confirmed victories in North Africa to his earlier score of one and one shared kills

Horbaczewski then scored his fifth kill on 2 April in EN315/ZX-6, but the mission flown four days later in EN459/ZX-1 was much more thrilling for him;

'When flying north at 10,000 ft, approximately ten miles south of Cekhira, Flt Lt Horbaczewski saw five Me 109s at the same height approaching from the east into the sun. He reported the enemy aircraft, but apparently his message was not received and he left his section to engage the Me 109s. He turned in behind the enemy aircraft, flying on the starboard side of a loose vic. A deflection shot from 200 yards was followed by a stern attack, closing in to 50 yards. There was an explosion in the Me 109 and the pilot bailed – the parachute did not open. At this point Flt Lt Horbaczewski's aircraft was hit by fire from another Me 109. He turned onto his back to bail out as the engine was on fire, but this manoeuvre appeared to put out the fire, so he righted the aircraft and glided to Gabes L/G [landing ground]. Aircraft Category 2 [aircraft can be repaired within second line servicing capability of the parent or nearest unit].'

Flt Lt Kazimierz Sporny in the cockpit of EN315/ZX-6 in early May 1943 after the sixth kill marking had been applied to the aircraft, denoting the Macchi C.202 credited to WO Popek on 28 April

Four more aces (or future aces) scored while flying with the PFT – Flt Lts Wacław Król and Kazimierz Sporny and WOs Mieczysław Popek and Kazimierz Sztramko. Oddly, Flt Lt Karol Pniak, the first Pole to achieve acedom in the Battle of Britain (his two 'Me 109s' on 18 August 1940 were his fifth and sixth kills), failed to score in Africa.

On 28 April WO Popek was credited with a Macchi C.202 destroyed as his fifth confirmed victory. His report shows clearly that by this stage of the campaign the real problem was not to shoot down an enemy aircraft, but to find a target that was not already being taken care of by someone else;

'I was flying with my section at 21,000 ft six miles southeast of Cape Bon when two MC.202s were reported at 15,000 ft on the port side, flying north. The section dived to attack. I fired from 250-300 yards but saw no results. We broke away, and as we were about to attack again 12 aircraft of 601 Sqn attacked the enemy aircraft and we were unable to get within range. I then saw a Mk VB Spitfire chasing an MC.202. I passed the Spitfire as I dived after the enemy aircraft, which veered east towards Pantellaria. I closed to 150 yards when about five-six miles northwest of the island after a chase lasting five minutes. I fired a long burst and saw pieces fly off as the enemy aircraft turned over onto its back and crashed into the sea.'

The 25 victories credited by the RAF to the PFT during two months of fighting made it the top-scoring fighter unit of the PAF in 1943, as it bettered the whole-year results of each squadron based in Britain.

At the end of the Tunisian campaign Wg Cdr Peter Olver, commanding No 244 Wing, signed the diary of the Polish unit with the following words;

'The Polish Combat Team joined the wing at Bu Grara, Tunisia, on 16 March 1943, became operational the following day and re-equipped with Spitfire Mk IXs, which it first used operationally on 25 March. During April the team obtained a higher score of enemy aircraft to their credit than any other flight or squadron in the wing. This speaks for itself as far as operations are concerned. We have been proud to fight with them, we have enjoyed living with them, and look forward to meeting them when peace comes.'

Reuter's release about the PFT's achievements in Africa, as quoted in the contemporary press

Polish Airmen Set Record Of 23 To 1

London, May 7.

A Polish fighter flight in Tunisia between March 17. when they went into action, and the end of April, shot down 23 Axis planes for certain. probably destoyed three, and damaged several, for the loss of one airman.

The proportion of 23 successes to one loss is a record in itself. The poles form a separate unit of experienced pilots.

(Reuter).

'HORBY'

With the fighting in North Africa over sooner than expected, the Polish pilots were invited to join RAF units in the area, rather than return to Britain as originally planned. Eventually, three of them accepted the offer. Sqn Ldr Skalski took command of No 601 Sqn soon afterwards, and Flt Lts Horbaczewski and Drecki were posted to Nos 43 and 152 Sqns,

Delivered to the PFT on 15 April 1943, EN355/ZX-0 was flown in combat by aces WO Popek and Flt Lt Horbaczewski during the next two days. However, on 18 April, Flg Off Mieczysław Wyszkowski was shot down in it and taken prisoner

respectively, as flight commanders. Sadly, Drecki was killed in a takeoff accident in September. Horbaczewski subsequently took command of No 43 Sqn in August, and led it until called back to Britain in October.

Since pre-war times this truly legendary pilot had been known to his close Polish friends by the nickname 'Dziubek', an informal and affectionate word for 'mouth' or 'a kiss', also used in the meaning of 'my darling' or 'honey' (contrary to some mistranslations, it does *not* mean 'little beak'). Only a very few good friends were allowed to call Horbaczewski 'Dziubek' to his face. As this nickname implied, he looked rather delicate, which required him to make up for what he lacked in appearance by his actions. This was certainly a contributing factor to his becoming a very dedicated fighter pilot. On the other hand, it was probably for the same reason that he was well known for troublemaking and his lack of discipline while with the PAF.

Having said that, during the many years the author has spent researching World War 2 Polish fighter pilots he has found no other ace who enjoyed such admiration and respect among his subordinates as Horbaczewski when he was commanding a flight and then a squadron. In part this was certainly because he was an outstanding pilot and a courageous commander, leading rather than sending his men into combat. It may also have been because, having earlier been a 'rogue pilot' himself in Britain, Horbaczewski knew first-hand which disciplinary measures were desirable and effective. He certainly was not a martinet.

Spitfire F IX EN267/ZX-5 was used by Polish aces Sqn Ldr Skalski, Flt Lts Horbaczewski and Sporny and WO Sztramko to claim victories in North Africa

New Zealander Sqn Ldr Jack Torrance (a flying officer at the time, who later commanded No 351 Sqn, which was comprised almost exclusively of Yugoslav personnel) recalled more than 50 years later;

'He came as "A" Flight commander at a time when many experienced pilots had become time-expired and been posted away. Morale was not particularly high, and "Horbie" immediately injected a new spirit of aggression and confidence firstly into "A" Flight and soon into the whole squadron. There was a great feeling of a new spirit in 43 Sqn. His first act when appointed CO was to lead a gaggle of 12 Spitfires on a training flight, put us all into line astern and, without warning, lead us into a formation loop. He also took individual pilots up for mock combats, and I consider him to have been the most accurate pilot of a Spitfire in my experience – he could perform aerobatics at a slower speed than any other pilot I knew.

'I admired him as a pilot and leader, and also as one of the few really fearless individuals I ever met. All in all I have never been more impressed with any human being in my life.'

And this is how he was remembered by Sqn Ldr Thomas E Johnson DFC (a flight sergeant at the time, he eventually retired from the RAF in June 1971);

'"Horby", as Horbaczewski was known to most of the aircrew and groundcrew alike in the RAF, was one of the few people who have stood out in my life. I admired him, he inspired me and I was fond of him as a person.

'Until Horby took over the squadron I had never heard the squadron song – "We are the fighting Forty-Three, up from Sussex by the sea. You can tell them all, that we fight or fall, in fighting Forty-Three". We all lived in tents, and that night the song rang out down through the officers and airmen lines.

'As a flight commander "Horby" trained us to fly as a fighting team and above all to have confidence and pride in our flying. I remember him saying "Never mind the sky, you stay in your position in the flight", and then to prove his point he led us all round in a loop. He did this later on with the whole squadron when he was the CO. Indeed, we were "Horby's boys".'

In his book *Green Kiwi Versus German Eagle*, Flt Lt J Norby King (a flying officer at the time) wrote;

'"Horby" is the proverbial new broom. From now on none of us must be in the Mess tent without a shirt on. We are to smarten up our formation flying, too. The first time he loops the loop with the squadron – without warning – it is a shambles. "Horby" also introduces us to Finger Four sections so that the squadron of 12 can manoeuvre easily and watch out for each other's tails while looking in towards the leader. Better cross cover. The RAF has always formated in four sections of three, or three sections of four in line astern, which has been cumbersome and a source of delight to the Jerries. "Horby" explains the Finger Four title by showing his hand flat on a table and declaring the finger nails the four aircraft positions. We struggle with it, have a brush with some Me 109s and end up in perfect formation – but the sections are a mile apart, and he says "Don't you like me? One minute I have a squadron and the next minute I have 12 Spitfires all over the sky". You are wrong there, mate – we would follow you to hell and gone.'

'Horby' scored three more confirmed victories while commanding No 43 Sqn. The first of these was on 4 September, described thus in the ORB;

The PFT's top-scorer was Flt Lt Eugeniusz Horbaczewski, with five German aircraft confirmed destroyed. Subsequently, he was one of three Poles who stayed on with RAF units in the Mediterranean. Horbaczewski added to his score on Spitfires with No 43 Sqn and then on Mustang IIIs with No 315 Sqn. While commanding the latter unit he failed to return from a 'Rodeo' mission on 18 August 1944

Spitfire Vs of No 43 Sqn taxi on a dusty airfield – probably Tusciano, near Salerno – in September 1943. Although of poor quality, this photograph is believed to show Spitfire VC MA345/FT-G in the background. Horbaczewski used this machine repeatedly between July and September, and he was flying it on 27 July when he shared in the destruction of an 'Me 109' that he never claimed, in favour of the other two pilots involved in the action

'0725-0900 hrs – 15 aircraft were on patrol over Messina area. When formation was ten miles east of Reggio two Me 109s were seen by the Spitfire IX section at 25,000 ft approaching from the northeast. Enemy aircraft turned northwest, and then seeing our aircraft opened fire on them and turned again to the northeast, diving vertically at a very high speed. Our aircraft gave chase, and one of the enemy aircraft was destroyed by Sqn Ldr E Horbaczewski (POL) at "deck level". Enemy aircraft crashed at Cittanova. No 2 of the Spitfire section chased the other Me 109 but could not get nearer than 1000 ft. Enemy aircraft was last seen flying northeast.'

On the 15th the ORB records;

'1135-1400 hrs – 12 aircraft carried out a patrol over "Peaches" beaches, Naples. Spitfire IXs saw two FW 190s ten miles north of Salerno flying south at 12,000 ft. These were chased for 40 minutes to the northeast, and Sqn Ldr E Horbaczewski (POL) fired at one of the enemy aircraft from 350-400 yards range from astern. Smoke poured from engine of FW 190 and strikes were seen by Flt Lt R Rayner. Enemy aircraft claimed as damaged.'

And then, the following day;

'1310-1435 hrs – six aircraft carried out a patrol in the Salerno area. 12 FW 190s were seen coming from the south at 5000 ft when our aircraft were over base and about to "pancake". These were successfully attacked and three of the enemy aircraft were destroyed, two by Sqn Ldr E Horbaczewski (POL), one by Flt Lt R Rayner and one of the FW 190s was damaged by Flg Off D C Deuntzer.'

The last-mentioned were 'Horby's' final Spitfire victories, raising his score to 11 enemy aircraft destroyed, and making him the top-scoring Polish pilot on the type. Although he was expected to take command of his old No 303 Sqn upon returning to Britain, he was eventually made commander of No 315 Sqn, which soon afterwards converted to North American Mustang IIIs. Under Horbaczewski's leadership, the unit became the top-scoring Polish squadron of 1944. He added to his own score as well until he failed to return from operations on 18 August. That, however, is quite another story.

CHAPTER SEVEN

TACTICAL AIR FORCE

In early 1944 Spitfire F IX MA299/ZF-E of No 308 Sqn was flown by aces Flt Lt Antoni Głowacki and WO Kazimierz Sztramko, among others. At the time the two Polish wings were converting to tactical operations against ground targets, with less and less opportunity to engage the Luftwaffe in the air. However, MA299 had seen plenty of aerial action during the summer and autumn of 1943, when it was used by No 303 Sqn as RF-E. Flt Sgt Aleksander Chudek used it to claim Fw 190s destroyed on 6 and 23 September ('Ramrods S.36' and '240'), the latter success being the last time a confirmed kill was credited to a Polish ace flying a Spitfire

Late 1943 saw a huge reorganisation of the Allied air forces to prepare them for the planned invasion. 2nd Tactical Air Force (TAF) was established, its role being to provide direct air support to the army. The Polish component of 2nd TAF originally included No 18 (Polish) Sector, which controlled the 1st and 2nd Polish Wings (No 131 and 133 Sqns, respectively, in 2nd TAF). Initially, their everyday tasks were little changed. In fact late September and October saw some intensive engagements with Luftwaffe fighters in defence of Allied bomber operations.

On 23 September Flt Sgt Aleksander Chudek of No 303 Sqn was credited with an Fw 190 destroyed while flying Mk IX MA299/RF-E during 'Ramrod 240';

'When I saw four FW 190s southeast of Le Treport at about 24,000 ft I dived to attack with my section. I selected one of these enemy aircraft and followed it down to about 9000 ft. I fired three long bursts from my cannon and machine guns from 600, 500 and 400 yards, respectively. After the last burst I noticed explosion in the enemy aircraft, and the FW 190 went straight down in flames. The combat took place about 20 miles northwest of Poix from 23,000 ft down to 9000 ft at 1615 hrs.'

This was the last confirmed kill credited to any Polish ace flying a Spitfire. The last claim of any category credited to a Polish ace in a Spitfire came a month later during 'Ramrod 283' on 24 October. In his report Flg Off Władysław Potocki of No 306 Sqn wrote;

Tour-expired fighter pilots and worn-out Spitfires were both employed in training. Flg Off Henryk Pietrzak (standing in the middle) had three confirmed kills on Spitfires when he was posted to the Polish Fighter School at No 58 OTU. In October 1943 he moved with the Polish school to No 61 OTU at Rednal, where this photograph was taken in October or November, showing him with his pupils by the side of a rather worn-looking UU-coded Spitfire I, IIA or VA. Pietrzak subsequently returned to operational flying and added substantially to his score flying Mustang IIIs

'Two FW 190s attempted to attack the second box of bombers from ahead and below. I dived to intercept, firing at one of them from port and above. He gave a long burst of machine gun fire from 430 yards and another burst of cannon and machine gun fire from 500 yards. No strikes were seen by our pilot, but according to assessment of combat film No 3515, hits and smoke were seen on the port wingtip. This enemy aircraft is, therefore, claimed as damaged.'

DOWN TO EARTH

The end of 1943 and the beginning of 1944 marked a gradual change in the role of the two wings, which now commenced flying dive-bombing missions in addition to their traditional fighter duties. Even though the wings included some leading PAF Spitfire aces, including Flt Lts Drobiński and Gładych as flight commanders in Nos 317 and 302 Sqns, respectively, and Plt Off Adamek in No 317 Sqn, none of them would claim any aerial successes in the virtual absence of engagements with the Luftwaffe.

In April 1944 the fighter wings moved to forward airfields in anticipation of their redeployment to liberated France. Initially, No 131 Sqn was led by the top-scoring Polish ace Wg Cdr Stanisław Skalski, but in early April he exchanged places with No 133 Wing's Wg Cdr Julian Kowalski. Shortly thereafter No 133 Wing welcomed No 129 Sqn as its third squadron and duly converted to Mustangs. No 131 Wing (Nos 302, 308 and 317 Sqns) eventually re-equipped with Spitfire LF IXs, and from then on it mostly operated in support of ground troops.

The PAF's two remaining fighter units at the time, Nos 303 and 316 Sqns, also undertook some ground-support operations, despite both being part of the Air Defence of Great Britain (ADGB). While No 316 Sqn soon converted to Mustang IIIs, No 303 Sqn, commanded at the time by ace Sqn Ldr Koc, continued to fly Spitfires until April 1945.

Even before the Normandy landings the Spitfires were employed on intensive ground-attack operations in an effort to soften up German

Sqn Ldr Wacław Król was the only Polish ace to score in five different campaigns – Poland in 1939, France in early 1940, the Battle of Britain, the offensive over Western Europe and North Africa. He commanded No 302 Sqn during the invasion in June 1944, but failed to add to his score. His personal Spitfire, LF IX MK716 at the time, was coded WX-L for Leader, as was the unit's tradition

defences in France. Such attacks were potentially costly, as Polish squadrons found out in late May. Ace Plt Off Adamek was lost to flak during a 'Ranger' operation on 18 May, and three days later a total of six Spitfires were hit by AA defences during 'Ramrod 905' – four were downed in France and two returned badly damaged. One of the downed pilots, Flt Lt Jan Kurowski of No 308 Sqn, was killed, and two, including ace Flt Lt Stanisław Brzeski, were captured by the Germans. Ace Flt Lt Józef Jeka, commanding No 308 Sqn's 'B' Flight at the time, had more luck;

'I left Chailey at 0730 hrs on 21 May 1944 in a Spitfire IX L [LF IX] on a "Rhubarb" operation against locomotives and road transport. Southwest of Abbeville the engine was hit by flak, and I was forced to make a crash-landing near Miannay. I saw Germans running towards me, so I blew up the IFF [identification friend or foe], took my parachute and Mae West and ran into the forest nearby. I met a woman who gave me directions to Abbeville and I set off, bypassing the town and staying the night with a Frenchman at Mareuil-Caubert.

'On 22 May 1944 I walked to Amiens, where I contacted a Frenchman who took me to Oissy for the night. Next day this man introduced me to a ticket collector who passed me on to some friends of his in Amiens. These people took my photograph for me. I was then taken to Flesselles, and from there to Flixecourt. Here, I was given an identity card and German *Ausweis* [identity card], and remained in Flixecourt until Allied troops arrived on 2 September 1944. There were seven other evaders in the village.'

Mass is held in a hangar at Northolt during No 317 Sqn's Squadron Day celebrations on 16 March 1944. Note that the Spitfire displays the code JH-Y on the fuselage, but boasts an N on the bottom cowling beneath the propeller spinner. Ace Flt Lt Drobiński's personal F IX, BS445/JH-Y, was damaged in an accident during gunnery practice at RAF Llanbedr on 26 February 1944, and BS508/JH-N was seriously damaged three days later in a collision with MA222 at the same location. Clearly, BS508's lower cowling panel was used to repair BS445 to enable it to be flown back to Northolt, but repainting had not yet been completed when this photograph was taken

After the invasion it became a standard procedure for all downed aircrew that they should not attempt crossing the frontline, but wait in hiding until the area was liberated by Allied troops.

On 20 June 1944 Wg Cdr Julian Kowalski narrowly missed becoming an ace during a patrol when he was leading No 317 Sqn. Flying his personalised LF IX ML419/JK, he claimed an Fw 190 probably destroyed. This was his fourth probable, to add to three and one shared kills and two damaged. According to his PCR he was positive that he had hit the Fw 190, but he did not follow it down, instead re-forming his squadron and resuming the patrol. Two of his pilots engaged in the same combat chose to follow their victims right to the ground, and both were credited with confirmed destroyed.

Between April and July 1944 the RAF's No 135 Wing also reported to No 18 (Polish) Sector. Because of this arrangement some documents for No 135 Wing were prepared in Polish during that period. The wing included Nos 222 (Natal), 349 (Belgian) and 485 (New Zealand) Sqns with Spitfire LF IXs, and was led by Wg Cdr Peter Simpson (an ace with a score of four and three shared destroyed, one probable and three damaged), who was succeeded by Wg Cdr Jan Zumbach in July.

At the time of the Normandy landings Gp Capt Aleksander Gabszewicz commanded No 18 (Polish) Sector of the 2nd TAF, which controlled three wings with nine squadrons – five Polish, two British, one New Zealand and one Belgian

When technically 'on loan to the PAF', pilots from the wing, including some aces, scored numerous victories. Sqn Ldr David Cox of No 222 Sqn added an Fw 190 damaged to his previous score of seven and one shared destroyed, six probables and four damaged, while New Zealander Flg

Gabszewicz had scored most of his victories with SZ-G coded Spitfires of No 316 Sqn. Indeed, from 1943 onwards all of his personal Spitfires were coded SZ-G and sported the No 316 Sqn badge, even if that unit was no longer part of his wing. Another motif applied on all of these aircraft was 'Boxer the Dog', originally designed by No 316 Sqn groundcrewman Cpl Wojciech Milewski. This is LF IX NH342, flown by Gabszewicz from early June until mid-October 1944

Off Johnny Houlton of No 485 Sqn scored one and one shared Ju 88s destroyed, two 'Me 109s' destroyed and another damaged out of his eventual total of five and two shared destroyed and four damaged. Notably, all of his victories over Messerschmitts mentioned above were scored in Spitfire LF IX ML407/OU-V, which survives today, known throughout the warbird fraternity as 'the Grace Spitfire'.

On the other hand, No 303 Sqn was part of No 142 Wing of the ADGB. New Zealander Wg Cdr Johnny Checketts, who led the wing, often joined the squadron on operations and sometimes flew one of its machines rather than his personal LF VC AB509/JMC (which carried No 303 Sqn's 'Kościuszko' badge besides other insignia). No 303 Sqn (and the whole wing) soldiered on flying the 'clipped, cropped and clapped' Spitfire LF Vs, the condition of these worn-out machines steadily deteriorating despite the efforts of the groundcrew, resulting in more losses to technical failures than to enemy action. On 23 June WO Aleksander Chudek failed to return from a patrol over the bridgehead in LF VB AB271/RF-F (built in 1941). He was the top-scoring Spitfire pilot of Polish squadrons in Britain (Horbaczewski had a higher Spitfire score, but most of his victories were claimed in the Mediterranean).

Spitfire F IX MH910/RF-G was the usual mount of Flt Lt Eugeniusz Szaposznikow when he commanded No 303 Sqn's 'A' Flight in the summer of 1944. He was an eight-victory Battle of Britain ace, but he never scored on Spitfires

Sqn Ldr Bolesław Drobiński walks away from an R-coded Spitfire with his hand on his head. It is not certain when this photograph was taken, but when he flew an armed reconnaissance in F IX EN367/RF-R on 4 November 1944 it was hit by flak and, according to the Operations Record Book, a piece of shrapnel gave him 'a blow on head'

In July No 303 Sqn re-equipped with F IXs, but these were not brand new either as they included some machines used by Northolt Wing squadrons more than a year earlier. In September Sqn Ldr Drobiński took over as the new commander, but even this seasoned ace and veteran of the unit failed to avert the bad luck as far as aerial victories were concerned. No 303 Sqn was destined to score no more kills.

During the first days of August No 131 Wing moved to French territory. In early September it passed through a number of airfields to follow the advancing frontline, and by mid-April 1945 it had arrived in occupied Germany. The wing's last major air combat was fought on the morning on 1 January 1945 during the German *Bodenplatte* attack on its home base at St Denis-Westrem, near Ghent in Belgium. The Wing HQ had planned a ground-attack operation against German targets for the morning, based on the same assumption as the *Bodenplatte* raid – that the enemy would be suffering from New Year's Eve hangovers, and thus be unable to defend themselves. The Polish Spitfires were up well before the Germans, and they returned from their raid to find Luftwaffe fighters attacking their home airfield.

In a short combat nearly 20 Fw 190s were despatched for the loss of two Polish pilots and a few Spitfires. Many more of their own aircraft were lost on the ground, but these were quickly replaced. However, because of the

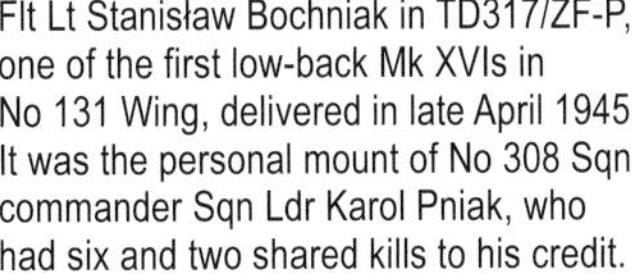

Flt Lt Stanisław Bochniak in TD317/ZF-P, one of the first low-back Mk XVIs in No 131 Wing, delivered in late April 1945. It was the personal mount of No 308 Sqn commander Sqn Ldr Karol Pniak, who had six and two shared kills to his credit.

Spitfire LF IX MK520 was involved in a very unusual plot at the end of World War 2 and just afterwards, when it became the first privately owned Spitfire, although not quite legally. Abandoned by the RAF at Rennes, in France, it was 'privatised' by ace Wg Cdr Tom Neil. By mid-1945 he had passed it on to Wg Cdr Marian Duryasz, Polish Liaison Officer (LO) at 2nd TAF/BAFO HQ. The Spitfire was serviced by No 131 Wing in Germany with the use of 'creative maintenance bookkeeping'. In early 1946 Duryasz left the Spitfire to Sqn Ldr Ludwik Martel, another Polish LO at the BAFO HQ. In May or June 1946 Martel traded the Spitfire to a USAAF officer for a substantial quantity of cigarettes. Thus, MK520 was the first Spitfire ever traded between individual people, with no official institutions being involved

timing of the Polish operation, none of the senior officers or aces of the wing took part in it – presumably because they had wanted to be able to participate fully in the preceding night's entertainment. So it was mostly up to young and relatively inexperienced pilots to score their first (and only) kills, rather than for the aces to add to their scores.

GET A SPITFIRE

Following VE Day, Polish fighter and bomber squadrons in Britain continued to train in their principal roles. After the British authorities withdrew recognition of the exiled Polish government in July 1945, the Polish Armed Forces (including the air force) came under British command, pending a decision as to their fate. It was only then that Polish Spitfire squadrons became part of the RAF.

In 1945 two Polish pilots were involved in an unlikely story of the world's first privately owned Spitfire. Probably due to a paperwork error, LF IX MK520 had been abandoned by the RAF at Rennes, in France, in the summer of 1944. It was 'privatised' there by ace Wg Cdr Tom Neil, at the time an RAF liaison officer to the 100th Fighter Wing of the USAAF (the story is described in detail in his book *The Silver Spitfire*, published in 2013). By mid-1945 he had given the aircraft away to Wg Cdr Marian Duryasz, Polish Liaison Officer at 2nd TAF HQ. Being based on the Continent with 2nd TAF and then British Air Forces of Occupation

Wg Cdr Wacław Król was one of the few Polish wing leaders whose Spitfires were marked with their initials. Low-back Mk XVI TD238 was coded WK-L, the 'L' standing for Loda, his fiancée. Here, LAC Jan Wawrzyczny is posing with it at Quakenbrück in 1946 (*Zbigniew Legierski collection*)

The end of the war meant, among other things, that ex-PoWs returned to service. At the beginning of 1946 Wg Cdr Stefan Janus was appointed Liaison Officer to No 11 Group HQ. He used Fighter Command Communications Squadron Spitfire LF IX MK994/N to visit the Polish wings at Coltishall and Hethel on 14 and 21 May 1946, respectively

(BAFO) HQ, Duryasz had the Spitfire serviced by No 131 (Polish) Wing in Germany, with the help of his friends there.

When, early in 1946, Duryasz was appointed to command a wing in the UK, he left the Spitfire to Sqn Ldr Ludwik Martel, Polish Liaison Officer at the BAFO HQ. By that time the aeroplane's armament had been removed, and the wing ammunition boxes were used to carry luggage. In February 1946 Martel was flying in a supply of cognac from France when one of the bottles broke while he was landing at Ahlhorn, and the smell of liquor filled the aeroplane. From then on his trips in it attracted too much unwanted curiosity at other airfields, and in May or June 1946 Martel traded the Spitfire to a USAAF officer for a substantial quantity of cigarettes. To this author's best knowledge MK520 thus became the first Spitfire ever to change hands in a commercial deal between two individuals, no official authorities being involved.

During 1946 all Polish squadrons were concentrated on several aerodromes in England, and they were eventually disbanded at the end of the year. As with all Polish servicemen in Britain, PAF personnel faced a dilemma – whether to return to their home country or stay abroad. They had gone to war to fight for an independent Poland, and this fight had been unsuccessful. It is estimated that of more than 14,000 men and women serving in the PAF at war's end, more than 11,000 remained abroad. The PAF was then reorganised into the Polish Resettlement Corps (RAF) to help those Polish airmen staying in the West to learn civilian trades.

Spitfire XVI TB292/QH-Z of No 302 Sqn at Warsaw-Okęcie airport in October 1945 after delivery to Poland's capital by Flt Lt Patrick Soutter for an RAF exhibition there. It had to be ferried by a British pilot because serving members of the exiled PAF were not allowed to set foot on Soviet-controlled Polish soil. The Spitfire was subsequently donated to the Polish Military Museum in Warsaw by the RAF, along with TB581/JH-Q of No 317 Sqn, but both were scrapped after a few years, being regarded as not 'politically correct' by the communists. Before the Warsaw trip TB292 had served with No 302 Sqn between February and October 1945. No Polish ace then serving with No 131 Wing flew it, but Sqn Ldr Dennis Usher, commanding No 274 Sqn, made at least two flights in the fighter. Notably, Wacław Król, No 131 Wing Leader at the time, had been a pilot with 'Skalski's Circus' in North Africa in 1943, during which time Usher scored most of his five kills with No 145 Sqn (*Robert Stachyra collection*)

A large number of PAF servicemen remained in exile, unable to return to communist-controlled Poland. Many of them joined the RAF in the post-war years, although it seems that only one Polish ace flew Spitfires during that period. Mirosław Wojciechowski resumed operational Spitfire flying with No 2 Sqn in Germany in 1949 on photo-reconnaissance PR XIXs, PM660/OI-X being one of his 'kites'. Although documentary corroboration is as yet lacking, it is not impossible that he flew spy missions across the 'Iron Curtain' and perhaps over his homeland (*Alfred Price collection via Peter Arnold*)

Many Poles joined the RAF, and some eventually reached high command positions. But as far as the author can ascertain, Mirosław Wojciechowski was the only Polish ace to fly Spitfires in RAF service after disbandment of the Polish squadrons. He then flew Gloster Meteor and Hawker Hunter jets, at one point having Gp Capt John Kent as his superior officer once again, until he was killed in a flying accident on 22 October 1956.

Seven other Polish aces served with the RAF post-war on flying or ground duties, but not on Spitfires. They were Stanisław Brzeski, Antoni Głowacki, Stefan Janus, Michał Maciejowski (who changed his name to Michael Manson), Władysław Potocki, Jerzy Radomski and Henryk Szczęsny. Radomski was the last of them to retire from the RAF, in August 1973.

Those who returned to communist-controlled Poland included some who joined the 'People's Air Force' upon arrival. The latter group included aces Stanisław Skalski and Kazimierz Wünsche. During the late 1940s/early 1950s a purge was carried out by the communist authorities, who removed those who had fought in the West from all aviation-related bodies (including banning them from amateur flying in aero clubs). Many were arrested and sentenced to death or long-term imprisonment, Skalski being among the latter. Wünsche escaped arrest and was 'only' discriminated against in various ways and finally expelled from the air force as a 'politically incorrect individual'.

It was not until Stalin's death and the 'thaw' of 1955-56 that veterans of the exiled Polish forces were able to resume normal life. In 1956 the PAF's

No details are known (to say nothing of documentary corroboration) of the alleged last-ever attempt by a Polish ace to use the Spitfire in combat. In 1961 three LF IXs, MH415, MK297 and MK923 (civil-registered in Belgium at the time as OO-ARD, OO-ARB and OO-ARF, respectively) were used in the filming of *The Longest Day*, bearing the spurious codes 'GW-R', 'GW-O' and 'GW-U'. Apparently, after the filming was completed, Jan Zumbach was involved in a deal to use them in the Katanga conflict. This was prevented by French authorities, who impounded them at Beauvais-Tille and despatched them instead by road back to Belgium on 10 January 1962. Here they are, awaiting their further fate, at Ostend in 1963, still in their *Longest Day* liveries but with Belgian civil registrations reapplied on their rudders (*Ron Cranham collection via Peter Arnold*)

Without the Spitfires, the mercenary pilots in Katanga had to make do with provisionally armed North American T-6 Texans. Jan Zumbach is third from the right in this photograph, which was almost certainly taken at Kolwezi airfield in 1962

new commander, Gen Jan Frey-Bielecki, invited them to join the PAF. Several outstanding fighter pilots accepted the offer, including the aces Wacław Król, Witold Łokuciewski, Stanisław Skalski and Stefan Witorzeńć. They undertook refresher flying training and conversion training onto jet fighters. Łokuciewski subsequently became the chief test pilot of the PAF's research establishment, while Witorzeńć formed and led an entirely new training centre for fighter pilots and commanders. Król and Skalski were given staff posts in the PAF HQ. Wünsche did not wish to rejoin the air force. Instead, he became one of the founders of Poland's modern air emergency medical service, and subsequently one of the pioneers of helicopter use in it.

A much less mysterious, although not necessarily less exciting encounter with the aircraft type they once flew – three aces of the exiled PAF and Spitfire XVI SM411 when it was officially unveiled at the Polish Aviation Museum in Cracow in 1977. They are, from left to right, Witold Łokuciewski, Stanisław Skalski and Wacław Król. Up to the present day, SM411 has been the sole Spitfire permanently based in Poland

One of the oldest surviving Spitfires flown by Polish aces, R6915, used by Tadeusz Nowierski in No 609 Sqn during the Battle of Britain, has been an Imperial War Museum exhibit for nearly 70 years. It is seen here undergoing restoration work at Duxford in September 2013 (*Peter Arnold*)

There was yet another group of ex-PAF members who continued to use their operational flying skills. A number of Polish flyers, including some fighter pilots, joined various clandestine organisations, either government sponsored or private. It is known that ace Józef Jeka flew in CIA-controlled operations, probably including dropping agents in communist countries. Contrary to what has been alleged in previous publications, however, it is unlikely that he ever flew the Lockheed U-2. He was killed in April 1958 during the civil war in Indonesia while working as the CIA-hired pilot of a Douglas B-26 Invader bomber. According to some researchers ace Bolesław Gładych was also involved in clandestine activities after the war, although these were not necessarily related to operational flying.

Probably the most prominent of this latter group, however, was Jan Zumbach. He took part in various secret and illegal activities, some of them flying. What matters most for this book is that in late 1961/early 1962 he was allegedly involved in an attempt to take several Spitfires to a 'private war' in Africa. Three LF IXs that had just been used in filming *The Longest Day* were apparently about to leave France for Congo-Katanga when they were impounded by French authorities. Zumbach and his comrades-in-arms eventually had to content themselves with provisionally armed North American T-6 Texans. It seems that from then on any further connection between Polish aces and Spitfires was only at airshows or in museums.

As regards the latter, MK923, one of the Spitfires that Zumbach tried to use operationally in the 1960s, has long been exhibited at the Museum of Flight in Seattle, Washington state. It is perhaps fitting, therefore, that when Bolesław Gładych passed away on 12 July 2011, as the last of the Polish aces, he died in Marysville, near Seattle – just around the corner from MK923.

APPENDICES

APPENDIX 1

POLISH ACES WHO FLEW SPITFIRES

Unlike the RAF, the exiled PAF prepared and published an official listing of victories credited to individual pilots. This was included in a document signed by Gp Capt Jerzy Bajan, the Senior Polish Liaison Officer to HQ Fighter Command, entitled *Polish Fighter Pilots Achievements During the Second World War* (1.9.1939 – 6.5.1945) [No. FC/S.5/1/AIR/CPLO.INTEL], dated 25 March 1946. This document provides the principal source for all victory credits quoted in this book. Where the figures have been amended by this author, the official figures are given in square brackets and explanatory comments are added below. Some of the pilots listed below were also credited with the destruction of V1s, but as no such claim was ever filed for a Polish pilot flying a Spitfire, they are not mentioned here.

LAST RANK	NAME	TOTAL SCORE	SPITFIRE SCORE
Flg Off	Mieczysław Adamek†	5+2sh/1/-	5/1/-
WO	Jakub Bargiełowski	5/-/3	-
Plt Off	Marian Bełc†	7/-/-	3/-/-
Flt Lt	Stanisław Blok	5/1/3	4/1/2
Flt Lt	Stanisław Brzeski	7+3sh/2/1	6+1sh/2/1
Flt Lt	Stanisław Chałupa	3+2sh/ 2/-	-
WO	Aleksander Chudek†	9/1/1	
Flt Lt	Michał Cwynar	5+1sh/1/-	3/-/-
Sqn Ldr	Bolesław Drobiński	7/1+1sh/-	
Wg Cdr	Jan Falkowski	9/1/-	8/1/-
Flt Lt	Mirosław Ferić†	9+1sh/1/-	1/-/-
Gp Capt	Aleksander Gabszewicz	8+3sh/1+1sh/3	7/1+1sh/2
Flt Lt	Bolesław Gładych	17/2/1sh [14/2/1sh][1]	7/2/1sh
Sqn Ldr	Antoni Głowacki	8+1sh/3/4	1sh/2/1
Flt Lt	Czesław Główczyński	5+1sh/2/1	1/-/-
Sqn Ldr	Władysław Gnyś	2+3sh/-/1	-
Sqn Ldr	Zdzisław Henneberg†	8+1sh/1/1	-
Sqn Ldr	Eugeniusz Horbaczewski†	16+1sh/1/1	11/1/1
Wg Cdr	Stefan Janus	6/-/1	
Sqn Ldr	Józef Jeka	7+1sh/-/3	2/-/1
Sgt	Stanisław Karubin†	7/-/-	-
Sqn Ldr	Tadeusz Koc	3+3sh/3/-	2+1sh/3/-
Flt Lt	Kazimierz Kosiński†	2+3sh/2/2sh	2/2/-
Plt Off	Jan Kremski†	3+6sh/1sh/4sh	2/-/-
Wg Cdr	Wacław Król	8+1sh/1+1sh/1sh	4/-/-
Sqn Ldr	Wacław Łapkowski†	6+1sh/-/1	4/-/1
Sqn Ldr	Witold Łokuciewski	8/3+1sh/-	3/2/-
Plt Off	Michał Karol Maciejowski	10+1sh/1/1 [9+1sh/1/1][2]	5+1sh/1/1
Wg Cdr	Mieczysław Mümler	4+3sh/-/1+1sh	-/-/1
Flg Off	Tadeusz Nowak†	4+1sh/1/1	1/-/-
Flt Lt	Eugeniusz Nowakiewicz	4+2sh/1/1	-
Wg Cdr	Tadeusz Nowierski	4+1sh/1/5 [3/1/6+1sh][3]	
Flt Lt	Adolf Pietrasiak†	7+4sh/-/2sh	7+1sh/-/-
Sqn Ldr	Henryk Pietrzak	7+1sh/1/1	3/-/1
Wg Cdr	Marian Pisarek†	11+2sh/1/2	5+1sh/1/-
Sqn Ldr	Karol Pniak	6+2sh/2/2+2sh	-
WO	MieczysławPopek†	3+2sh/-/2	

Sqn Ldr	Jerzy Popławski	5/-/2	
Sqn Ldr	Władysław Potocki	4+2sh/-/1	-/-/1
Flt Lt	Jerzy Radomski	2+3sh/1sh/4	1/1sh/3
Wg Cdr	Kazimierz Rutkowski	5+1sh/2/1	5/1/-
Wg Cdr	Stanisław Skalski	18+2sh/2/4+1sh	8/2/2
Flt Lt	Grzegorz Sołogub	5/1/-	3/1/-
Flt Lt	Kazimierz Sporny	5/1/1	4/-/-
Flg Off	Franciszek Surma†	6/2+1sh/1	5/1/-
Flt Lt	Eugeniusz Szaposznikow	8+1sh/-/1	-
Sqn Ldr	Henryk Szczęsny	8+3sh/1/2	6+1sh/-/1
WO	Kazimierz Sztramko	4+1sh/-/-	3+1sh/-/-
Gp Capt	Witold Urbanowicz	17/1/-	-
Sqn Ldr	Marian Wesołowski†	2+4sh/-/1+4sh	2/-/1
Gp Capt	Stefan Witorzeńć	5+1sh/-/2	-
WO	Mirosław Wojciechowski	4+1sh/-/-	1/-/-
Flt Lt	Kazimierz Wünsche	4+1sh/1/-	1+1sh/-/-

Notes

1) The 14 kills credited to Gładych officially by the PAF did not include three German aircraft destroyed in 1944 when he flew with the USAAF. One of these was erroneously categorised by the PAF as 'destroyed on the ground', while two others, confirmed by USAAF authorities, were achieved when Gładych was no longer considered as being in active service with the PAF.

2) An air-to-air kill achieved by Maciejowski when flying with No 249 Sqn was erroneously categorised by the PAF as 'destroyed on the ground'.

3) RAF documents as late as 1941 credited Nowierski with five German aircraft destroyed and two shared destroyed while flying Spitfires with No 609 Sqn between August 1940 and February 1941. The score was downgraded in PAF records to three destroyed, one probable and 6.5 damaged. However, researchers have traced the identities of German aircraft actually downed in at least two engagements for which Nowierski was only credited with 'damaged'.

† – killed during World War 2.

APPENDIX 2

KNOWN NON-POLISH ACES WHO FLEW SPITFIRES WITH POLISH UNITS

RANK WHEN FLYING POLISH SPITFIRES	NAME	POLISH SPITFIRE UNIT(S)	TOTAL SCORE	SCORE ON POLISH SPITFIRES
Wg Cdr	John Milne Checketts (NZ)	No 303 Sqn	14/3/8	-
Gp Capt	Arthur Hay Donaldson (British)[1]	No 303 Sqn	3+2sh/1+1sh/5	-
Capt	Francis Gabreski (US)	No 315 Sqn	34+1sh/1/5	-
Sqn Ldr	Colin Falkland Gray (NZ)[1]	No 315 Sqn	27+2sh/7+4sh/12	-
Wg Cdr	Kenneth Holden (British)	No 316 Sqn	5+1sh/1/5	-
Wg Cdr	John Alexander Kent (Canadian)	Nos 303 and 308 Sqns	12/3/3	4/-/-[2]
Flt Lt	Michael Plaistowe Kilburn (British)[3]	No 316 Sqn	6+1sh/-/4	-
Flt Lt	Gareth Leofric Nowell (British)[3]	No 316 Sqn	10+1sh/5/-	-
Sqn Ldr	Dennis Charles Usher (British)[1]	No 302 Sqn	5/-/2	-
Wg Cdr	Edward Preston Wells (NZ)[1]	No 316 Sqn	12/4/6+1sh	-

Notes

1) Officers at various command and staff posts who used Spitfires of Polish units for non-operational flying.

2) Kent's total score while flying aircraft of Polish units was 8/2/1, which includes Hurricane victories with No 303 Sqn in the Battle of Britain.

3) Members of No 124 Sqn (based at Northolt and equipped with high-altitude Spitfire F VIIs for air defence), who occasionally joined No 316 Sqn on offensive operations over the Continent during August 1943.

APPENDIX 3

POLISH AIR FORCE SPITFIRE UNITS

NAME[1]	ROLE	PERIOD	DEPLOYMENT
No 302 Sqn 'City of Poznań'	day fighter	October 1941 to August 1944	Britain
		August 1944 to October 1946	Continent
		October 1946 to December 1946	Britain
No 303 Sqn 'City of Warsaw'/'Tadeusz Kościuszko'[2]	day fighter	January 1941 to April 1945	Britain
No 306 Sqn 'City of Toruń'	day fighter	June 1941 to April 1944	Britain
No 308 Sqn 'City of Cracow'	day fighter	April 1941 to August 1944	Britain
		August 1944 to October 1946	Continent
		October 1946 to December 1946	Britain
No 315 Sqn 'Dęblin'[3]	day fighter	July 1941 to April 1944	Britain
No 316 Sqn 'City of Warsaw'	day fighter	October 1941 to April 1944	Britain
No 317 Sqn 'City of Wilno'	day fighter	October 1941 to August 1944	Britain
		August 1944 to October 1946	Continent
		October 1946 to December 1946	Britain
No 318 Sqn 'City of Gdańsk'	fighter-reconnaissance	December 1943 to April 1944	Middle East
		May 1944 to August 1946	Italy
		August 1946 to December 1946	Britain
Polish Fighting Team (also known as the Polish Combat Team or simply 'C' Flight, No 145 Sqn RAF)	day fighter	March 1943 to May 1943	North Africa

Notes

1) Fighter squadrons of the exiled PAF (except No 315 Sqn) were named after major Polish cities.

2) The original 'Kościuszko Squadron' was formed by American volunteers during the Polish-Russian war of 1920 (in a similar manner to the *Escadrille La Fayette* formed in France during World War 1) and named after Tadeusz Kościuszko, a Polish military leader of the 18th Century who was also a general in the American War of Independence. The 'Kościuszko Squadron' traditions were continued by a Warsaw-based fighter unit until 1939, and were then resurrected by No 303 Sqn in Britain. Today they are still maintained by the 23rd Tactical Air Base of the PAF.

3) Unlike all other PAF fighter squadrons, No 315 Sqn was named after the small town of Dęblin, the seat of the PAF College from 1927 to date.

APPENDIX 4

POLISH AIR FORCE SPITFIRE WINGS

Squadrons were rotated regularly to provide alternative periods of intensive operations and rest. From October 1943 the 1st and 2nd Polish Wings were known as Nos 131 and 133 Airfields/Wings within the 2nd TAF structure. The 3rd Wing was an operational force in the summer of 1943, and then in 1945 (on Mustangs). During the intervening period it existed merely as a PAF administrative structure controlling the remaining fighter squadrons.

	1st POLISH WING (No 131 AIRFIELD/WING WHILE WITH 2nd TAF)	2nd POLISH WING (No 133 AIRFIELD/WING WHILE WITH 2nd TAF)	3rd POLISH WING
1/4/41 to 24/6/41	No 303 (No 306 on Hurricanes)		
24/6/41 to 13/7/41	Nos 303, 308 (306 converting from Hurricanes)		
14/7/41 to 7/10/41	Nos 306, 308, 315		
7/10/41 to 13/12/41	Nos 308, 315, 303	Nos 316, 317, 302 (converted from Hurricanes in October)	
13/12/41 to 1/4/42	Nos 315, 303, 316	Nos 317, 302, 306	
1/4/42 to 5/5/42	Nos 303, 316, 317	Nos 302, 306, 308	
5/5/42 to 16/6/42	Nos 303, 316, 317, 302	Nos 306, 308, 315	

16/6/42 to 30/7/42	Nos 316, 317, 302, 306	Nos 308, 315, 303	
30/7/42 to 5/9/42	Nos 317, 302, 306, 308	Nos 315, 303, 316	
5/9/42 to 1/2/43	Nos 302, 306, 308, 315	Nos 303, 316, 317	
1/2/43 to 11/3/43	Nos 306, 308, 315, 303	Nos 316, 317, 302	
12/3/43 to 29/4/43	Nos 308, 315, 303, 316	Nos 317, 302, 306	
29/4/43 to 1/6/43	Nos 315, 303, 316	Nos 302, 306, 308	
1/6/43 to 20/6/43	Nos 303, 316, 302, 317	Nos 306, 308, 315	
20/6/43 to 6/7/43	Nos 303, 316	Nos 306, 308, 315	Nos 302, 317
6/7/43 to 21/9/43	Nos 303, 316	Nos 306, 308	Nos 302, 317
21/9/43 to 11/11/43	Nos 303, 302, 317	Nos 308, 306	
11/11/43 to 15/3/44	Nos 302, 317, 308	Nos 306, 315	
15/3/44 to 30/4/45	Nos 302, 317, 308	Nos 306, 315, 129* (converted to Mustang IIIs in April 1944)	
30/4/45 to circa 1/7/45	Nos 302, 317, 308, 322*, 349*		
circa 1/7/45 disbandment	Nos 302, 317, 308		
* Non-Polish squadrons			

APPENDIX 5

POLISH ACES WITH RAF SPITFIRE SQUADRONS DURING WORLD WAR 2

No 43 Sqn – Eugeniusz Horbaczewski (flight commander July-August 1943 and squadron commander August-October 1943)
No 54 Sqn – Stanisław Blok (April-May 1942)
No 65 Sqn – Bolesław Drobiński (August 1940-March 1941)
No 72 Sqn – Kazimierz Kosiński (July-November 1941) and Jerzy Radomski (August-November 1941)
No 74 Sqn – Henryk Szczęsny (August-December 1940)
No 92 Sqn – Adolf Pietrasiak (June-July 1941)
No 145 Sqn (other than the Polish Combat Team) – Kazimierz Kosiński (July 1941)
No 164 Sqn – Stanisław Blok (May-July and November-December 1942)
No 222 Sqn – Jerzy Radomski (November-December 1942)
No 504 Sqn – Stanisław Blok (October-November 1942)
No 601 – Eugeniusz Horbaczewski (June-July 1943); Stanisław Skalski (pilot June-July 1943 and squadron commander July-October 1943)
No 603 Sqn – Stanisław Blok (March-April 1942)
No 609 Sqn – Tadeusz Nowierski (August 1940-March 1941)
No 611 Sqn – Antoni Głowacki (October-November 1941)
Moreover, Aleksander Gabszewicz (as No 18 Sector Commander) and Jan Zumbach (as No 135 Wing Leader) flew on operations with No 349 Sqn in May and July 1944, respectively.

APPENDIX 6

SURVIVING SPITFIRES KNOWN TO HAVE BEEN FLOWN BY POLISH ACES

Mk I
P9306 – Henryk Szczęsny (with No 74 Sqn)
P9444 – Mieczysław Mümler and Jan Zumbach (both with No 58 OTU)
R6915 – Tadeusz Nowierski (with No 609 Sqn)
X4590 – Tadeusz Nowierski (with No 609 Sqn)

Mk II
P7819 – Bolesław Drobiński, Zdzisław Henneberg and Witold Urbanowicz (all with No 303 Sqn)

Mk V
P8746 – Aleksander Gabszewicz (as a guest with No 308 Sqn)
BL655 – Stanisław Blok (with No 164 Sqn)
BM597 – Stanisław Blok and Aleksander Chudek (with No 315 Sqn)

Mk IX
BR601 – Kazimierz Rutkowski and Stefan Witorzeńć (both as guests with No 316 Sqn)
BS410 – Stanisław Blok and Michał Cwynar (with No 315 Sqn)
EN179 – Michał Cwynar (with No 315 Sqn), Władysław Potocki (with No 306 Sqn), Władysław Gnyś and Michał Maciejowski (both with No 316 Sqn)
MH434 – possibly Stanisław Blok (with No 84 Group Support Unit)
ML407 – possibly Karol Pniak (with No 308 Sqn)

Mk XIX
PM627 – Mirosław Wojciechowski (with No 2 Sqn)
PS915 – Mirosław Wojciechowski (with No 2 Sqn)

Notes
1) P8208 and X4590 were not flown by any of the numerous aces serving with No 303 Sqn when these Spitfires were used by the unit in 1941.
2) BL246 was not flown by any Polish aces while used by No 316 Sqn from early June until late November 1942. However, during its time with No 316 Sqn it was repeatedly flown by ace Wg Cdr Ken Holden. Notably, BL246/SZ-A was the regular mount of Sqn Ldr Janusz Żurakowski (whose final official score was 3/1/1), who later gained worldwide fame as an outstanding test and display pilot. After the war 'Zura' test-flew another surviving Spitfire, two-seat Mk VIII trainer MT818/G-AIDN.
3) It has been claimed that Spitfire LF IX MJ783 was flown by Aleksander Gabszewicz with No 302 Sqn, but this has proved impossible to corroborate with documents.

COLOUR PLATES

1
Spitfire I R6631/PR-Q of Flg Off Tadeusz Nowierski, No 609 Sqn, Middle Wallop, August-September 1940

Flg Off Tadeusz Nowierski flew this Spitfire on two occasions. On 24 August he was at its controls during a mission described in the No 609 Sqn diary as follows; 'Squadron was ordered to intercept raiders over Ryde, and found themselves 5000 ft below a large formation of bombers and fighters, right in the middle of our own AA fire, and down-sun. The squadron was attacked and fortunate to sustain no further casualties other than two aircraft damaged.' Nowierski's R6631 was one of those two. On other occasions Plt Off Michael Appleby and Flg Off John Curchin both claimed victories in this Spitfire. It was lost along with Plt Off Paul A Baillon on 28 November 1940 during the epic combat in which two famous aces, Flt Lt John Dundas and Major Helmut Wick, were killed.

2
Spitfire I R6775/YT-J of Plt Off Bolesław Drobiński, No 65 Sqn, Tangmere, November 1940-January 1941

Spitfire I R6775/YT-J was flown during August 1940 by Jeffrey Quill, Supermarine's principal test pilot, who joined No 65 Sqn to gain combat experience on the type. A few months later R6775 was the usual mount of Plt Off Bolesław Drobiński, a future Polish Spitfire ace. Initially, it continued to carry the markings of the Battle of Britain period, as shown here, but towards the end of 1940 it received the new Fighter Command quick-recognition items – the Sky spinner and band on the rear fuselage, plus the Night (black) port wing undersurface. Transferred to No 54 Sqn in February 1941, the Spitfire then soldiered on with various RAF units and establishments until it was finally struck off charge in August 1944.

3
Spitfire IIA P7859/RF-V of Sgt Marian Bełc, No 303 Sqn, Northolt, March-April 1941

Delivered brand new to No 303 Sqn, P7859 became the usual mount of Sgt Bełc, who already had four confirmed victories to his credit and was destined to add three more later that year in Mk IIB and Mk VB Spitfires. An early Mk IIA, P7859 had its Sky band around the fuselage applied incorrectly at No 38 Maintenance Unit (MU), aligned with the slanting fuselage/tail joint. The black undersurface of the port wing was another quick-recognition feature introduced in late 1940. It was discontinued in April 1941. Typically for No 303 Sqn at the time, the Spitfire displayed the squadron emblem under the windscreen, but featured no PAF marking. This particular machine had a very short operational career as it was lost on 20 April 1941 when Sgt Matěj Pavlovič, one of several Czechs who chose to fly with the exiled PAF, was shot down and killed during a 'Sphere' operation.

4
Spitfire IIA P8038/RF-W of Sqn Ldr Witold Urbanowicz, 1st Polish Wing, Northolt, 26 April 1941, and Plt Off Bolesław Drobiński, No 303 Sqn, Northolt, 15 May 1941

Delivered brand new to No 303 Sqn and usually flown by Flg Off Wojciech Kołaczkowski, this Spitfire made history in the hands of two other pilots, both outstanding aces. Sqn Ldr Urbanowicz, a 15-kill ace of the Battle of Britain, was appointed to command the 1st Polish Wing on 1 April 1941. On 26 April he flew P8038 when he led the wing (No 303 Sqn on Spitfires and No 306 Sqn on Hurricanes) for an uneventful patrol between London and Hastings, this being the first-ever wing-strength operation by Polish squadrons. On 9 May Urbanowicz flew a 'Sphere' sortie in the same Spitfire. Six days later Plt Off Drobiński was at the controls of P8038 during a 'Rhubarb' operation when he claimed his first enemy aircraft – a Ju 52/3m damaged on the ground at St Inglevert aerodrome, shared with Sgt Marian Bełc in P8099/RF-V. Within two months Drobiński was credited with six enemy aircraft destroyed in aerial combat, becoming the Polish top-scorer on Spitfire IIs. In May 1941 P8038 was transferred to No 452 Sqn, becoming the usual mount of Flt Lt 'Paddy' Finucane, previously Drobiński's colleague in No 65 Sqn, who then used it to claim three and two shared Bf 109s destroyed plus a probable. This Mk IIA proved very long-lived, serving with the RAF until September 1945.

5
Spitfire VB R7195/QJ-B of Sgt Adolf Pietrasiak, No 92 Sqn, Biggin Hill, 8 July 1941

Built in February 1941, R7195 was originally given the presentation name *HOLMEWOOD I*. It was one of the first Mk VBs in operational service, with No 92 Sqn. The *EAST INDIA SQUADRON* inscription was applied on all Spitfires of the unit during that period. On 8 July 1941 Sgt Adolf Pietrasiak flew R7195 during 'Circus 39', when he was credited with an 'Me 109F' destroyed. This success took his score to three and four shared destroyed. The Spitfire was also used to good effect by future ace Plt Off Philip Archer, who claimed 'Me 109s' destroyed on 23 June and 9 July. However, on the latter occasion he was wounded and the aeroplane seriously damaged in combat. Repaired, the Spitfire remained in operational use until 1943, when it was modified into an LF VB. R7195 was then delivered to No 501 Sqn, and it served until shot down over France on 24 March 1944, its pilot, Canadian Plt Off Frank Vid, being killed.

6
Spitfire IIA P7919/ZF-Y of Flg Off Tadeusz Nowak, No 315 Sqn, Northolt, 16 July 1941

This aircraft was in the first batch of Spitfire IIs delivered to No 308 Sqn, all of which had previously served with No 611 Sqn. The previous unit's FY code was crudely overpainted before the application of No 308 Sqn's ZF in smaller characters. This is the earliest known Spitfire with its aircraft letter expanded into a girl's name (in this case *Ywonia*, 'Polish-ed' form of Yvonne) – this practice subsequently became widespread in Polish squadrons. As far as can be ascertained, during 1941 No 308 Sqn Spitfires were adorned with the PAF white-and-red square on the nose, but no squadron badge. In mid-July 1941 pilots of No 315 Sqn, recently deployed to Northolt, flew aircraft of Nos 306 and 308 Sqns to acquaint themselves with the type. On 16 July Flg Off Tadeusz Nowak, whose score at the time was three and one shared kills, failed to lock the undercarriage of P7919 down before landing, resulting in serious damage being inflicted on the fighter. The pilot was unhurt. Following repairs, the Spitfire served with various RAF units until November 1944.

7
Spitfire VB AB930/ZF-J of Flt Lt Stefan Janus and Flg Off Franciszek Surma, No 308 Sqn, September-November 1941

This aircraft was delivered brand new to Northolt when the 1st Polish Wing converted from Mk IIs to Mk Vs. Allocated to No 308 Sqn, it became the usual mount of Flt Lt Stefan Janus, who used it to score a double victory during a sweep on 24 October. It was also flown on occasion by Flg Off Surma, who was credited with a Bf 109 destroyed on 16 September. However, during 'Circus 110' on 8 November the latter pilot was shot down and killed in AB930 off Dunkirk.

8
Spitfire VB AB914/PK-Z of Sgt Michał Cwynar, No 315 Sqn, Northolt, 16 September 1941

Another Mk VB delivered brand new to Northolt during conversion to the variant, AB914 was used during a sweep on 16 September by Sgt Michał Cwynar to claim an 'Me 109' probably destroyed. Similarly to No 308 Sqn, No 315 Sqn did not apply the squadron badge on its Spitfires at the time, merely carrying the PAF marking on the nose. On 3 October this Spitfire was seriously damaged in a landing accident whilst being flown by another pilot. Following repairs it was returned to service with No 315 Sqn as PK-R. AB914 then served with No 317 Sqn as JH-S until it was written off in a crash-landing on 1 December 1942.

9
Spitfire VB W3798/ZF-Y of Sqn Ldr Marian Pisarek, Flt Lt Marian Wesołowski and Flg Off Jerzy Popławski, No 308 Sqn, Northolt, September-December 1941

Yet another Spitfire VB delivered brand new to Northolt in early September 1941, W3798 was used to good effect by three aces of No 308 Sqn. Flt Lt Marian Wesołowski was the first of these, being credited with an 'Me 109' probably destroyed during 'Circus 101' on 21 September 1941. On 13 October 1941 Sqn Ldr Marian Pisarek, commanding No 308 Sqn, claimed an 'Me 109' destroyed during 'Circus 108A'. These proved to be the final victories claimed by Wesołowski and Pisarek. Flg Off Jerzy Popławski then used the Spitfire to damage an 'Me 109' during 'Circus 110' on 8 November 1941. A week later the same pilot, returning from the 'Ramrod 10' operation, had a landing accident in W3798 that resulted in the fighter suffering serious damage. Following repairs it served with No 316 Sqn, and Plt Off Czesław Jaworowski used the fighter to down an Fw 190 on 3 May 1942. The aircraft subsequently served with a number of squadrons before eventually becoming ground instructional airframe 4263M in October 1943.

10
Spitfire VB AD350/JH-S of Sqn Ldr Henryk Szczęsny, No 317 Sqn, Exeter, October-December 1941

One of the first Spitfire VBs delivered brand new to No 317 Sqn when the 2nd Polish Wing converted from Hurricanes in October 1941, AD350 was selected by Sqn Ldr Henryk Szczęsny as his personal mount. It was duly adorned with his nickname, *Hesio*, under the cockpit, and two white swastikas on the nose, denoting his two shared kills scored with No 317 Sqn. The unit's Spitfires usually displayed both the PAF square on the nose and the squadron badge, which at the time was applied on a pale blue diamond background immediately aft of the cockpit. In early January 1942 Szczęsny chose BL543 as his new JH-S, and AD350 was recoded JH-F. It was written off during the disastrous 'Roadstead 12' on 15 March 1942, when No 317 Sqn lost ten of its aircraft in crash-landings in mist. The pilot, Flg Off Jerzy Mencel, escaped unhurt.

11

Spitfire VB W3424/JH-Q of Sgt Stanisław Brzeski, No 317 Sqn, Exeter, November 1941-April 1942

A fairly early Spitfire VB from Supermarine production, W3424 was originally delivered to No 616 Sqn in July 1941. Following an accident and repairs, it went to No 317 Sqn, becoming the regular mount of Sgt Stanisław Brzeski. On 6 December 1941, he used it to claim a Ju 88 destroyed over Plymouth Sound, thus becoming an ace with three and two shared destroyed enemy aircraft. Similar to many other Spitfires of No 317 Sqn, W3424 displayed a victory marking, presumably denoting Brzeski's kill on 6 December, and a personal name, *Sheila*, under the windscreen. Among other occasions, Brzeski flew this Spitfire during the fateful 'Roadstead 12', when he was one of just two pilots who landed safely despite the appalling conditions. W3424 was written off in an accident in May 1942 while still with No 317 Sqn.

12

Spitfire VB AA872/UZ-S of Flg Off Stanisław Skalski, No 306 Sqn, Northolt, December 1941-February 1942

Delivered brand new to No 316 Sqn in October 1941, when the entire 2nd Polish Wing converted to Spitfire VBs, AA872 was coded SZ-X. In mid-December 1941 it was transferred, along with all of No 316 Sqn's aircraft, to No 306 Sqn, and the fighter was eventually recoded UZ-S. AA872 then became the personal mount of 'B' Flight commander Flt Lt Stanisław Skalski, who at the time had 12 and two shared kills to his credit, including four on Spitfires. Although No 306 Sqn normally applied both its badge and the PAF marking to its aircraft, it seems that for some reason AA872 displayed only the latter. On 9 February 1942 Skalski overshot the runway at Bolt Head and hit a bowser trailer. Following repairs the Spitfire was allocated to the Fleet Air Arm (FAA), becoming a 'hooked Spitfire'. It was lost on 25 October 1942 in a landing accident with 885 Naval Air Squadron on HMS *Formidable*, killing its pilot, Kiwi Sub Lt J D Houston.

13

Spitfire VB BL646/SZ-R of Flt Lt Stanisław Skalski, No 316 Sqn, Northolt, 10 April and 3 May 1942

At the beginning of March 1942 Flt Lt Skalski was posted to command 'B' Flight of No 316 Sqn. He chose this newly delivered brand-new Mk VB as his personal mount. It is not known why he did not have it coded SZ-S for 'Skalski', but chose the aircraft letter R instead (when he later commanded No 317 Sqn his Spitfire was coded JH-Q). A presentation Spitfire, BL646 was funded by Prins Bernard Fond and named *Muntok* after a town in the Dutch East Indies. Typically for No 316 Sqn it was adorned with the PAF square on the nose and the squadron badge aft of the cockpit. Skalski scored two victories in the Spitfire, an Fw 190 destroyed during a 'Rodeo' on 10 April and another probably destroyed during 'Circus 145 (repeated)' on 3 May. This Spitfire was used by No 316 Sqn until late 1942, and then, following some repairs and modification to LF VB standard, it was returned to the unit in late 1943. Having served with a number of RAF units, BL646 was sold to Portugal in 1947, where it received the serial number 44.

14

Spitfire VB AA913/RF-P of Plt Off Antoni Głowacki, No 303 Sqn, Northolt, 27 April 1942

This Spitfire originally went to No 72 Sqn in November 1941. Following an accident and repairs it was delivered to No 303 Sqn, where in late April and early May 1942 it was often flown by Plt Off Antoni Głowacki, an ace with eight kills to his credit (including five scored on 24 August 1940 in a No 501 Sqn Hurricane). On 27 April Głowacki used this Spitfire to claim an Fw 190 probably destroyed during 'Circus 141'. AA913 was also repeatedly flown in No 303 Sqn by another ace, Flg Off Bolesław Gładych. Later used by No 302 Sqn as WX-X, AA913 was eventually converted into a 'hooked Spitfire' and transferred to the FAA, serving until May 1945.

15

Spitfire VB BL563/JH-M of Flg Off Tadeusz Koc, No 317 Sqn, Northolt, 28-29 April 1942

This aircraft was delivered brand new to No 317 Sqn in early January 1942. It is not clear if the small-size roundels were applied at No 6 MU or by the Polish squadron. During April and May 1942 BL563 was usually flown by Flg Off Tadeusz Koc, who scored three victories in it – an Fw 190 during 'Circus 144' on 28 April, followed by a second Fw 190 destroyed and a third probably destroyed the following day during 'Circus 145'. While with No 317 Sqn the Spitfire was also flown by a number of other aces, namely Flt Sgts Brzeski, Maciejowski and Sztramko, as well as Sqn Ldr Nowierski from the Wing HQ. It was later used by several other frontline units, and in early 1945 BL563 was transferred to the French air force.

16

Spitfire VB AD198/RF-J of Wg Cdr Stefan Janus, 1st Polish Wing, Northolt, May 1942

This Spitfire was initially issued to No 403 Sqn. It was damaged in December 1941, and following repairs the fighter was delivered to Northolt for the personal use of the wing leader. The serial number was applied in a non-standard position on the fuselage during the post-accident repair. The newly appointed Wg Cdr Janus had AD198 coded RF-J, since No 303 Sqn was responsible for the maintenance of the 'WingCo's' machine. Janus used it until the end of the month, when he switched to another Spitfire, and AD198 was allocated for normal squadron use (see profile 19).

17

Spitfire VB BM531/RF-V of Flg Off Bolesław Gładych, No 303 Sqn, Northolt, May-June 1942

Delivered brand new to No 303 Sqn in early May 1942, this aircraft became the usual mount of ace Flg Off Bolesław Gładych, who flew it regularly during May and June. Gładych's tally was applied under the unit badge in the form of five black crosses with white outlines (destroyed) and one with a red outline (probable). The Spitfire was also flown by other aces while with No 303 Sqn, namely Flg Off Jerzy Radomski, Plt Off Antoni Głowacki and WO Mirosław Wojciechowski. Wg Cdr Stefan Janus, the Northolt Wing Leader, used BM531 as his personal Spitfire during the first week of June 1942 before he chose EN916 as his new mount. BM531 continued to be used by No 303 Sqn until June 1943 when, with all other Mk Vs, it was transferred to No 315 Sqn. The fighter was written off in an accident on 2 September 1943 whilst still serving with the unit.

18

Spitfire VA W3114/FJ-K of Plt Off Stanisław Blok, No 164 Sqn, Skaebrae, May-July 1942

This was one of the first Spitfire Vs, built in May 1941 and delivered the following month to No 54 Sqn. By early 1942 the Mk VA variant with its cannon-less armament was quite obsolete for use against Luftwaffe fighters. In January 1942 W3114 was allocated to No 332 (Norwegian) Sqn at Catterick and then, in April, to No 164 Sqn at Peterhead, from where it was quickly deployed to Skaebrae, in the Orkneys. This unit was one of the so-called 'Gift Squadrons', its aircraft originally being funded by the Argentine Patriotic Fund, which contributed £100,000. For this reason the unit's badge showed the British lion superimposed on Argentina's rising sun, and all of its aircraft were marked *ARGENTINE (BRITISH)*. Between May and July 1942 W3114/FJ-K was repeatedly flown by Plt Off Stanisław Blok, one of several Polish pilots posted to the unit at the time (apparently to 'cool down'). On 31 May 1942 the aeroplane was being flown by Plt Off W J Cleverly when he and Blok (in R6801) shared in damaging the Ju 88 credited to No 164 Sqn as its first aerial combat success. In September 1942 W3114 went to No 602 Sqn at the same location. From 1943 the veteran fighter was used by No 61 OTU until late 1944, when it was struck off charge.

19

Spitfire VB AD198/RF-W of Flt Sgt Mieczysław Adamek and Flg Off Bolesław Gładych, No 303 Sqn, Northolt, June-July 1942

Following its use as the wing commander's mount (see profile 16), AD198 was allocated to 'B' Flight of No 303 Sqn during early June 1942. The fighter became the new mount of Flt Sgt Adamek, replacing AB906 (which had been sent away for repairs), and so it received his 'lucky' letter W. Although Adamek flew AD198 throughout June and July 1942, he failed to score with it. Flg Off Gładych, who flew this Spitfire on only three occasions, was, however, credited with an Fw 190 in it during 'Circus 188B' on 5 June, this being his last confirmed kill with No 303 Sqn. On 27 June the Spitfire was damaged in an accident and sent away for repairs. It then served with a number of squadrons and was eventually converted into an LF VB. In mid-February 1944 AD198 was reallocated to No 303 Sqn, only to be written off in a landing collision on 15 March.

20

Spitfire VB BL549/WX-E of Plt Off Eugeniusz Nowakiewicz, No 302 Sqn, Northolt, 23 July 1942

After being delivered brand new to No 302 Sqn in February 1942, BL549 was selected by Sqn Ldr Julian Kowalski as his personal mount and, in accordance with the unit's tradition, coded WX-L for 'Leader'. At the beginning of June Kowalski chose a new Spitfire, EN865, as his next WX-L, and BL549 was conveniently recoded WX-E. Typically for No 302 Sqn at that time, the aircraft displayed its PAF square under the cockpit and no squadron badge. Ace Plt Off Nowakiewicz flew only two operational sorties in it, but the second of these, a 'Rhubarb' over France on 23 July, proved to be the most fateful of his career. He was shot down by flak near Foret de Boulogne and initially managed to evade capture with the help of local Polish immigrants, but he was eventually arrested by the Gestapo. Nowakiewicz spent several months incarcerated in the infamous Fresnes prison, south of Paris, before finally being transferred to a PoW camp.

21

Spitfire VB BL690/JH-Z of Flt Lt Kazimierz Rutkowski, No 317 Sqn, Northolt, 19 August 1942

This Spitfire was delivered factory fresh to No 317 Sqn in mid-March 1942, in the wake of the disastrous 'Roadstead 12'. Coded JH-Z, it was the usual mount of the 'B' Flight commander, initially Flt Lt Marian Duryasz and then ace Flt Lt Kazimierz Rutkowski. The latter was at the controls of BL690 on 19 August when he was credited with a Do 217 destroyed at about 1030 hrs. The Spitfire displayed typical markings for this period, including the squadron badge, which in 1942 began to be applied under the cockpit, without the diamond-shaped background. In early September 1942 BL690 was transferred to No 315 Sqn when the two units switched stations and aircraft. In December it went to No 308 Sqn, with whom the fighter was subsequently damaged in an accident on 1 May 1943. Following repairs, BL690 was supplied to Portugal in late 1943, receiving serial number 19.

22

Spitfire VB BL927/JH-L of Plt Off Michał Maciejowski, No 317 Sqn, Northolt, 19 August 1942

This aircraft spent nearly two years of its service life with Polish units. Delivered to No 317 Sqn as another replacement after the unfortunate mission of 15 March, it became the usual mount of Plt Off Lech Xiężopolski. During Operation *Jubilee* on 19 August it was flown by three different pilots on three sorties, one of them being Plt Off Maciejowski, who was credited with a Do 217 shared destroyed at about 1630 hrs. BL927 then served consecutively with Nos 315, 308, 306 and 316 Polish Sqns until January 1944. It was struck off charge by the RAF in December 1945.

23

Spitfire F IX BS241/UZ-J of Wg Cdr Stefan Janus, 1st Polish Wing, Northolt, October 1942-January 1943, and Plt Off Henryk Pietrzak, No 306 Sqn, Northolt, 9 October 1942

Delivered to Northolt in October 1942, BS241 was duly selected by Wg Cdr Janus as his new mount. Like all of Janus' previous aircraft it was not marked in any special way as the wing commander's machine. As the fighter was allocated for maintenance purposes to No 306 Sqn, it was coded UZ-J. In line with No 306 Sqn practice at the time, the Spitfire displayed the unit badge under the cockpit and the PAF square on the nose. Although it was normally flown by Janus or his deputy, Sqn Ldr Tadeusz Nowierski, other pilots flew BS241 on occasion. On 9 October 1942 ace Plt Off Henryk Pietrzak used it when he was credited with an Fw 190 destroyed during 'Circus 224'. On 26 January 1943 Janus was at the controls of the Spitfire during 'Circus 256' when he collided with his wingman over the Channel. He spent the rest of the war as a PoW.

24

Spitfire F IX BS463/UZ-G of Plt Off Henryk Pietrzak, No 306 Sqn, Northolt, October-December 1942

This Spitfire was delivered factory fresh to No 306 Sqn in late September 1942. During October and the first half of November it was regularly flown by Plt Off Henryk Pietrzak prior to him being posted to the Aeroplane and Armament Experimental Establishment to take part in the testing of the Spitfire XII. His sorties in BS463 included 'air cover' for the goalless England versus Scotland football match at Wembley on 10 October. In March 1943 the aircraft was transferred to No 316 Sqn, which traded places with No 306 Sqn, taking over its aircraft. Now coded SZ-G, it was usually flown by Flg Off Maciejowski, but another ace, Flt Lt Falkowski, had an accident in it. After further movements, in 1944 BS463 ended up with No 303 Sqn, where it was flown by ace Sqn Ldr Bolesław Drobiński, among others. It then went to No 441 Sqn RCAF and eventually to No 80 (French) OTU, being struck off charge in January 1946.

25

Spitfire F IX BS411/PK-I of Plt Off Stanisław Blok, No 315 Sqn, Northolt, December 1942-May 1943

First flown in late October, this Spitfire was delivered to No 315 Sqn in early November 1942. From late December 1942 until the end of May 1943 it was frequently flown by Plt Off Stanisław Blok, and on 13 May he flew BS411 during 'Ramrod 71', when he was credited with an Fw 190 damaged. At the beginning of June 1943 it was transferred to No 303 Sqn, along with all of No 315 Sqn's Spitfires. Coded RF-I, the fighter was flown by various pilots, including aces Flt Lt Koc and WOs Wünsche and Popek. On 11 November No 308 Sqn took over all of the Spitfire IXs operated by No 303 Sqn up to that time, and BS411 was recoded ZF-I. Eight days later it was force-landed at Lisieux by Flg Off Frąckiewicz, who was captured by the Germans.

26

Spitfire VB W3765/WX-F of Flg Off Bolesław Gładych, No 302 Sqn, Heston/Kirton-in-Lindsey/Hutton Cranswick, December 1942-May 1943

Originally delivered to No 306 Sqn at Northolt in September 1941, this Spitfire passed to No 303 Sqn a month later when the two units exchanged aircraft and bases. It became the personal mount of Sqn Ldr Kołaczkowski, coded RF-K and sporting the names *Krysia* (added to the aircraft letter) and *Wojtek* (on the cowling). Damaged in an accident on 13 March 1942, W3765 was sent away for repairs and, after a period of storage, was delivered to No 302 Sqn at Heston in December 1942. Coded WX-F, it became the usual mount of Flg Off Bolesław Gładych, who flew the fighter frequently until early May 1943. In March 1943 W3765 was also flown on several occasions by Wg Cdr Aleksander Gabszewicz, leading the 2nd Polish Wing. In June it was transferred to No 308 Sqn. Eventually converted into an LF VB, the Spitfire then served with a number of RAF squadrons until it was struck off charge in July 1945.

27

Spitfire VB BL594/WX-G of Wg Cdr Aleksander Gabszewicz, 2nd Polish Wing, Kirton-in-Lindsey/Hutton Cranswick, February-May 1943

Delivered to No 242 Sqn in April 1942, BL594 was damaged in an accident in May, repaired and delivered to No 303 Sqn at Kirton-in-Lindsey, becoming the personal mount of Flg Off Horbaczewski, coded RF-G. After he left No 303 Sqn in September, BL594 was flown by a number of pilots, including aces Flt Lt Drobiński, Flg Off Głowacki and WO Popek. In early February 1943 the Spitfire was left behind at Kirton when No 303 Sqn moved to Heston. Later that month it became the personal aircraft of Wg Cdr Gabszewicz. Finished in standard No 302 Sqn markings, with the unit badge under the windscreen, the fighter displayed the pilot's score – seven-and-a-half black crosses (which does not match the number of kills credited to him at the time, but might have referred to all categories of his claims in Britain) – and the name *Smarkata* (roughly equivalent to 'Chit', referring to his very young fiancée, Elisabeth Helen Bullimore). At the beginning of June No 302 Sqn moved to the 1st Wing at Heston and BL594 was left behind in No 308 Sqn's care. Soon afterwards Wg Cdr Gabszewicz became the wing leader at Northolt, and BL594 remained with No 308 Sqn. It was then converted into an LF VB, and in January 1944 the aircraft went to No 234 Sqn. It was lost on operations while being piloted by Flg Off D N Greenhalgh on 9 May 1944.

28

Spitfire F IX EN300/ZX-9 of WO Kazimierz Sztramko, Polish Fighting Team ('C' Flight, No 145 Sqn), Bu Grara/La Fauconnerie/Goubrine, Tunisia, March-April 1943

Like all Spitfires of the PFT, EN300 was not assigned to any particular pilot. Flt Sgt Sztramko, who achieved 'acedom' while in North Africa, flew this aircraft on several occasions in March and April, but failed to score in it. In line with all other aircraft of the PFT, EN300 displayed the code letters ZX of No 145 Sqn, plus a numeral – 9 in this case – instead of an aircraft letter. In April it was used by two non-ace pilots to score two confirmed kills – WO Bronisław Malinowski on the 7th and WO Władysław Majchrzyk on the 20th – so it is possible that two white swastikas were painted near the cockpit on the port side (available photos show that the Polish national marking and the kill symbols were applied only to the port side of the unit's Spitfires). Used by the PFT until late May, EN300 was then transferred to No 1 Sqn South African Air Force. It was shot down off Catania on 14 July by USAAF P-38 Lightnings in a 'friendly fire' incident. Its pilot, Lt M E S Robinson, bailed out safely and was picked up.

29

Spitfire F IX BS403/SZ-K of Flg Off Michał Maciejowski, No 316 Sqn, Northolt, 11 June 1943

Delivered new to No 306 Sqn in late October 1942, BS403 became the personal mount of the unit's commander, Sqn Ldr Kazimierz Rutkowski, with the code UZ-K. On 11 March 1943 No 316 Sqn exchanged bases and aircraft with No 306 Sqn, and BS403 was recoded SZ-K and became the usual mount of Plt Off Jerzy Szymankiewicz. It was flown by other pilots as well, including aces Gp Capt Mümler, Flt Lts Falkowski and Gareth Nowell (No 124 Sqn) and Flg Off Maciejowski. The last-named was the sole pilot to score a victory in this Spitfire with No 316 Sqn when he was credited with an 'Me 109' destroyed during 'Rodeo 229' on 11 June 1943. On 9 August that same year the aircraft was seriously damaged during a training sortie and sent away for repair. BS403 then served with a number of RAF units until it was sold to France in July 1946. Despatched to Indochina, the Spitfire saw operational use there but its ultimate fate is unknown.

30

Spitfire VC JK539/FT-C of Flt Lt Eugeniusz Horbaczewski, No 43 Sqn, Pachino, Sicily, August 1943

Delivered to the RAF in March 1943, this Spitfire was shipped to the Mediterranean in April and arrived on Malta at the end of May. Supplied to No 43 Sqn, it was flown from Pachino airfield, in southern Sicily, by Flt Lt Horbaczewski (among others) in the first days of August 1943. Horbaczewski subsequently commanded No 43 Sqn for two months, from August until October 1943. At least until the Allied landings on the Italian mainland the aircraft was still finished in the Desert scheme. The underside colour is shown as Azure here, but it might have been Light Mediterranean Blue. Following operational service JK539 was delivered to the Air

Gunnery and Bombing School (Middle East) at El Ballah, in Egypt, where it was written off in an accident on 4 July 1945.

31

Spitfire F IX MH349/SZ-X of Gp Capt Mieczysław Mümler, 1st Polish Wing, Northolt, August-October 1943

Built in July 1943, MH349 was delivered to Northolt in mid-August. Coded SZ-X, it became the usual mount of the two station commanders, Gp Capt Maurice W S Robinson (RAF) and Gp Capt Mieczysław Mümler (Polish). At that time the SZ code was not only worn by No 316 Sqn aircraft but also by a number of aeroplanes allocated to the Northolt Station Flight. Spitfire MH349 replaced Gp Capt Robinson's earlier SZ-X, Mk VB BL479, and continued to be used by the senior officers at Northolt after Robinson was replaced by Gp Capt Frederick E Rosier and Mümler by Gp Capt Tadeusz Rolski. When Gp Capt Aleksander Gabszewicz replaced Rolski at the head of No 18 Sector in March 1944, he used MH349 as his personal Spitfire, recoded SZ-G. In May he switched to MJ451, and MH349 was taken over by Wg Cdr Julian Kowalski (No 131 Wing Leader) and recoded again, this time with his initials JK. When the entire wing converted to the LF IX, MH349 went to No 274 Sqn. It then served with a number of other units until the fighter was written off on 10 February 1945 during a post-inspection check flight by Miles test pilot Walter Gustav Capley, who was killed in the crash.

32

Spitfire F IX MA222/RF-A of WO Mieczysław Popek, No 303 Sqn, Northolt, 3 October 1943

Delivered brand new to No 315 Sqn in mid-May 1943, MA222 was coded PK-O and flown by ace Flg Off Stanisław Blok, among others. At the beginning of June it was transferred, with all the other aircraft of the unit, to No 303 Sqn, which replaced No 315 Sqn at Northolt. Recoded RF-A, the fighter was flown by a number of pilots, including aces Flt Lt Wacław Król, Plt Off Kazimierz Wünsche, WO Mieczysław Popek and Flt Sgt Aleksander Chudek. Popek flew it during 'Ramrod 259' on 3 October when he claimed an Fw 190 damaged in what eventually proved to be No 303 Sqn's last successful aerial combat. On 11 November the Spitfire went to No 308 Sqn, which replaced No 303 Sqn at Northolt and took over its aircraft. It was recoded ZF-A and was then used as the personal mount of the 'A' Flight commander, ace Flt Lt Antoni Głowacki. On 29 February 1944 MA222 was damaged in the hands of a No 317 Sqn pilot, although it is not clear whether the Spitfire had been transferred to that unit or had just been borrowed for this particular sortie. Following repairs it was allocated to No 229 Sqn, and after the war the Spitfire was delivered to the French air force. It is known to have served at the training centre at Meknes, in Morocco, until at least 1950.

33

Spitfire VC AB212/UZ-V of Flg Off Władysław Potocki, No 306 Sqn, Heston, 24 October 1943

A presentation Spitfire named *Lancastria Avenger III*, AB212 was first flown in December 1941 and served with a number of units before it was delivered to No 306 Sqn in October 1943. The aircraft was flown by various pilots, and on the 24th Flg Off Potocki flew it during 'Ramrod 283', claiming an Fw 190 damaged as his first victory, to which he would later add four and two shared kills in Mustangs. Potocki's damaged claim in AB212 was the last aerial success credited to any Polish ace flying a Spitfire. Following an accident in late January 1944, and consequent repairs, the Spitfire was transferred to No 133 Wing's sister unit, No 315 Sqn. Recoded PK-C, it was flown by various pilots, including another future Mustang ace, Sgt Jakub Bargiełowski. In April the unit converted to Mustang IIIs, and its Spitfires went to second-line units – AB212 ended up with No 53 OTU until it was struck off charge in 1945.

34

Spitfire LF IX MH883/WX-O of Flt Lt Grzegorz Sołogub, No 302 Sqn, B61 St Denijs-Westrem, Belgium, October-December 1944

This Spitfire was delivered in October 1943, going to No 412 Sqn RCAF. Coded VZ-B, it was the personal mount of the famous ace Flt Lt George 'Buzz' Beurling, who used it to score his last victory – an Fw 190 destroyed on 30 December 1943. Damaged in combat in April 1944, MH883 was repaired, and in October of that year it was delivered to No 302 Sqn in France. Ace Flt Lt Grzegorz Sołogub tested it on delivery on 18 October and chose the fighter as his usual mount. After he was reposted to become a flight commander with Mustang-equipped No 306 Sqn in England, MH883 was flown by various pilots, but most often by Flt Sgt Stanisław Celak. On 1 January 1945 he had the annoying experience of being shot down by trigger-happy 'friendly' AA gunners during the German *Bodenplatte* attacks, but fortunately he escaped unhurt. The aircraft was repaired and eventually sold to Turkey in 1947. Allocated serial 6220, it was, however, written off on delivery there.

35

Spitfire LF XVI TD240/SZ-G of Gp Capt Aleksander Gabszewicz, No 131 (1st Polish) Wing, B101 Nordhorn and B113 Varrelbusch, Germany, April-June 1945

One of the early low-back Mk XVIs, TD240 was the very first of the type in No 131 Wing (the aircraft was delivered on 20 April 1945). It was little wonder, therefore, that it became the personal machine of Gp Capt Gabszewicz. As with his previous Mk IX and XVI Spitfires, it was coded SZ-G and given the rank pennant and 'Boxer the Dog' personal emblem. Gabszewicz used it until his departure in mid-June to become the station commander at RAF Coltishall. TD240 was then taken over by No 302 Sqn commander, Sqn Ldr Bolesław Kaczmarek. Unlike all his predecessors in the post, Kaczmarek had his Spitfires coded with his 'lucky' letter rather than WX-L, so TD240 became WX-V and had the name *Janetka* (a pseudo-Polish form of Janet) applied forward of the cockpit, although Gabszewicz's dog was not obliterated. Kaczmarek allowed other pilots to use his mount occasionally, and on 10 October 1945 WO Kazimierz Chomacki wrote it off in a crash-landing.

36

Spitfire PR XIX PM627/OI-X of WO Mirosław Wojciechowski, No 2 Sqn, Wunstorf/Bückeburg, West Germany, December 1949-February 1951

Mirosław Wojciechowski was almost certainly the last Polish ace to fly Spitfires. Joining the RAF post-war, he underwent a refresher course on Mk XVIs and was posted to No 2 Sqn in Germany to fly PR XIXs. Between December 1949 and February 1951 he flew PM627 OI-X more than 30 times. In 1951 the Spitfires were replaced by Meteors in No 2 Sqn, and PM627 was sold to India in 1953, serving until 1957. Preserved in a museum collection there, it was then traded to Canada in 1971, and in the 1980s the aircraft went to the *Flygvapenmuseum* (Swedish Air Force Museum) at Malmen, near Linköping, where it has been displayed ever since.

BIBLIOGRAPHY

The information in this book is based on wartime documents held at the Polish Institute and in the Sikorski Museum Archives, London (mostly personal files of fighter pilots, and various fighter squadron and Wing-level documents, all in LOT.A.V.44 to LOT.A.V.55 series), and at The National Archives in Kew (mostly personal combat reports in the AIR 50 series and squadron Operations Record Books in the AIR 27 series), as well as those in the author's personal archive.

The following books and websites were also consulted;

Boot, Henry, and Sturtivant, Ray, *Gifts of War. Spitfires and other Presentation Aircraft in Two World Wars*, Air Britain, 2005

Brown, Alan, *Airmen in Exile. The Allied Air Forces in the Second World War*, Sutton Publishing, 2000

Gretzyngier, Robert, *Poles in Defence of Britain*, Grub Street, 2001

Gretzyngier, Robert, Matusiak, Wojtek, and Zieliński, Józef, *Polish Air Force Aces*, Bellona, 2012

Halley, James J, *Royal Air Force Aircraft EA100-EZ999*, Air Britain, 1988

Halley, James J, *Royal Air Force Aircraft JA100-JZ999*, Air Britain, 1990

Halley, James J, *Royal Air Force Aircraft P1000-R9999*, Air Britain, 1996

Jefford, C G J, *RAF Squadrons*, Airlife, 1994

King, J Norby, *Green Kiwi Versus German Eagle*, self-published, 1991

Królikiewicz, Tadeusz, and Matusiak, Wojtek, *Polski samolot i barwa. Polskie Siły Powietrzne na Zachodzie 1940-1946 (Polish Aircraft and Colour. Polish Air Force in the West 1940-1946)*, Bellona/Instytut Lotnictwa, 2014

Matusiak, Wojtek, *303 Squadron – The Complete Illustrated History Vols 1-3*, Red Kite, 2014-15

Matusiak, Wojtek, *306 Dywizjon Myśliwski Toruński (306 'City of Toruń' Squadron)*, Bellona, 2003

Matusiak, Wojtek, *Polish Wings 6: Supermarine Spitfire I-II*, Stratus, 2007

Matusiak, Wojtek, *Polish Wings 13: Supermarine Spitfire IX 1942-1943*, Stratus, 2011

Matusiak, Wojtek, *Polish Wings 15: Supermarine Spitfire IX 1944-1946*, Stratus, 2012

Riley, Gordon, Arnold, Peter, and Trant, Graham, *Spitfire Survivors Then and Now Vols I-II*, A-Eleven Publications, 2010-13

Shores, Christopher, and Williams, Clive, *Aces High Vol 1*, Grub Street, 1994

Shores, Christopher, *Aces High Vol 2*, Grub Street, 1999

Shores, Christopher, *Those Other Eagles*, Grub Street, 2004

Sturtivant, Ray, and Hamlin, John, *RAF Flying Training and Support Units since 1912*, Air Britain, 2007

Terbeck, Helmut, van der Meer, Harry, and Sturtivant, Ray, *Spitfire International*, Air Britain, 2002

Thomas, Andrew, *Osprey Aircraft of the Aces 98 - Spitfire Aces of North Africa and Italy*, Osprey, 2011

www.britmodeller.com

www.mysliwcy.pl

www.polishairforce.pl

www.thegazette.co.uk

INDEX

Note: locators in **bold** refer to illustrations, captions and plates.